Hiking Ten

"A thoroughly revised, useful guide to outdoor recreation in the Volunteer State."

—*Chattanooga Times*

"A delightful guide for meandering through the wonders of Tennessee's wilderness and urban areas . . . useful information concerning the length of the trail, degree of difficulty, access points, parking areas, camping sites and points of current or historical interest . . . required reading for anyone interested in hiking or backpacking in Tennessee."

—*The Leaf-Chronicle,* Clarksville, Tenn.

"Covers almost every official trail in the state and a good portion of those on private land."

—*Buffalo River Review,* Linden, Tenn.

"The historical backgrounds of the trails and their development are fascinating . . . an excellent traveling companion for the experienced hiker . . . recommended highly."

—*The Oak Ridger,* Oak Ridge, Tenn.

Hiking Tennessee Trails

Fourth Edition

by
Evan Means

edited by
Bob Brown

An East Woods Book

The Globe Pequot Press

Old Saybrook, Connecticut

Computerized maps rendered by Mary Ballachino from hand-drawn originals submitted by Alan Stokes.

Library of Congress Cataloging-in-Publication Data

Means, Evan.
    Hiking Tennessee trails / by Evan Means. — 4th ed.
        p. cm.
    "An East Woods book."
    Rev. ed. of: Tennessee trails. c 1989.
    ISBN 1-56440-377-7
    1. Hiking—Tennessee—Guidebooks. 2. Trails—Tennessee—
Guidebooks. 3. Tennessee—Guidebooks. I. Means, Evan. Tennessee
trails.
    II. Title.
GV199.42.T2M4 1994
796.5'1768—dc20
                                                        93-39425
                                                        CIP

Manufactured in the United States of America
Fourth Edition/First Printing

Contents

List of Maps

Acknowledgments

This book could not have been produced without the help and encouragement of many people. We express our sincere thanks to those who made this effort possible: to Grimes Slaughter, a past president of Tennessee Trails Association, who needled contributors to get their assignments done and whose topographical maps were indispensable; to the other officers of TTA and the members who contributed; and to Chancellor Bob Brandt and Joe Gaines, who furnished background material.

We could not have completed this project without the support and cooperation of the U.S. Forest Service, the Tennessee Valley Authority, and the Tennessee Department of Conservation. State trails system administrator Harry Williamson and trail coordinators Mike Dahl, Bob Richards, and David Shupe all went out of their way to help. We thank David Stidham, recreation planner for the U.S. Army Corps of Engineers and chairman of the Nashville Chapter of TTA, for handing out assignments and keeping his group working. Special thanks to Clarence Streetman and David Rhyne of Bowater Southern Paper Corporation for their encouragement. Thanks also to Molly Killingsworth for her excellent editing job. A pause in memory of those old-timers Paul Fink and Paul Adams, and special thanks to B. W. Chumney, who provided historical information about Cherokee National Forest. The author appreciates the help of the TTA people who assisted in bringing this book up to date, including Bob Barnett, president; Bob Brown, whose enthusiasm inspired me to start the first edition; and the folks in the Memphis, Murfreesboro, and Nashville chapters. Thanks to state parks personnel and the staffs of the Big South Fork and the Cherokee National Forests.

I give an extra hug to my dear wife, Virginia, who served as proofreader and critic and helped keep my nose to the typewriter (and word processor) when I would rather have been fishing. And thanks to Liz and Ernie Collins and to the Andrews family for keeping an eye on the house when we were "on the trail."

Editor's Acknowledgments

The editor wishes to thank those individuals who contributed trail descriptions for the current and previous editions of this work: Mike Dahl for Overmountain Victory Trail, Emilie E. Powell for Cumberland Trail Section 9, Stan Gorin for Shellsford-Cardwell Mountain Trail, Donald Todd for Frozen Head State Park and Natural Area trails, George Minnigh for Pickett State Park trails, Jack Neff for Fall Creek Falls State Park trails, Bill Hager for Cedars of Lebanon State Park, Russell Fryer for Montgomery Bell State Park, John Hart for Nathan Bedford Forrest State Park, Ken Humphreys for Fort Pillow State Historical Area, Debbie Gilbert for Meeman-Shelby Forest Day Use Park, Randy Hedgepath for South Cumberland State Recreation Area, Jerri Bull for Fisherville Nature Trail, Dot Ventress for Lookout Mountain, Judith Bartlow for River Bluff and Big Ridge trails, Harold Draper for Hemlock Bluff National Recreation Trail, David Stidham for Bearwaller Gap Trail, Bertha Chrietzberg for Twin Forks Trail, Deborah Beazley for Percy and Edwin Warner parks, and Clarence Streetman and David Rhyne for Bowater Pocket Wilderness trails.

Grateful acknowledgment is also given to those who revised existing trail descriptions or provided new information for this edition: Jack Coleman, Sam Powell, Bob Richards, Alan Wasik, John Howell, Billy Glenn Smith, Stuart Carroll, Billy Martin, Kenny Daniel, Bill Troup, Jim Nash, Jim Harrison, Brenda Coleman, Charles Spearman, Todd Yann, Rob Turan, Terry Chilcoat, Jerry Conley, and Art Hamman.

The editor is also grateful to Alan Stokes for the significant improvement to the maps. Mr. Stokes redrew every map with clarity and presented detail as well, making this edition that much more helpful to readers.

Finally, it was an honor to be asked by Evan Means to revise this little volume, his labor of love for almost two decades.

Introduction

Before we completed the inventory, we had a dream of including all the trails in Tennessee in one volume. When the count reached 283 outside the Smokies and we were still counting, it became apparent that our dream was impractical. We have tried to describe the best hiking trails, distributed from east to west, since that is the direction taken by the explorers and settlers who crossed the Appalachian Mountains from Virginia and the Carolinas. The Appalachian Trail and Great Smoky Mountains National Park are not included in this guide, since a large number of guidebooks cover those areas. We recommend *Hiking in the Great Smokies* by Carson Brewer, available at park visitor's centers, and *Walks in the Great Smokies* by R. and P. Albright (from The Globe Pequot Press). Guidebooks for the Appalachian Trail area available from the Appalachian Trail Conference, P.O. Box 807, Harpers Ferry, West Virginia, 25425; the Sierra Club also has some excellent guidebooks.

There are more than a hundred hiking trails listed on the map "Trails of the Cherokee National Forest." These range in length from 0.2-mi. interpretive trails in recreation areas to 138 miles of the Appalachian Trail. Hikers also have access, at their risk, to fourteen motorcycle, thirteen horse, and six bicycle trails. Obviously, we couldn't include all of them, so we have picked out some of the best. There are many good trails in state parks, but again, we selected a few good trails and left out some of equal quality.

We had many pleasant experiences while doing field research. We walked through Cumberland Gap with Daniel Boone and followed his footsteps along Walden Ridge. We followed the paths of the Indians along the crest of the Appalachians and camped beside tumbling mountain streams. In our mind's eye, we followed David Crockett on bear hunts in the canebrakes along Tennessee rivers and carried corn to his gristmill at Crockett Falls on Shoal Creek in Lawrence County. We watched squirrels romp in a hollow oak tree, then climbed Big Ridge, where Indians ambushed and scalped the pioneer Peter Graves in 1794. We marveled at the views of the great "gulfs" carved by nature from the Cumberland Plateau and rested in rock houses, great overhanging rock formations that have sheltered hunters and hikers for centuries. We hope that the reader will share these experiences with us and find other adventure on Tennessee trails.

There is very little flat land in Tennessee, and most of the trails are rocky to a certain extent. We recommend sturdy hiking shoes that protect the ankles. A light staff is essential to maintain balance on precipitous paths, aid in climbing and descending steep slopes, and serve as a probe when crossing logs and rocks that might harbor dangerous snakes. Temperatures vary widely over a twenty-four-hour period, so plan your clothing accordingly. The clothing layers peeled as you climb a mountain slope will feel good when put back on at the top. Nights are cool in the mountains, so arrange to sleep warmly. We assume that most readers have reference material on camping and backpacking equipment, so we shall not bore you with further instructions. Good hiking!

Hiking Tennessee Trails

1. Historical Background

When they crossed the Appalachians into the upper Tennessee Valley in the middle of the sixteenth century, Hernando de Soto and later Juan de Pardo found, and utilized an elaborate system of trails established by Indian traders from the Ohio Valley to Florida and the lower Mississippi River. A party, which penetrated the Cherokee country from Virginia in 1673, found Spanish trade goods, even though they were the first white men most of the Indians had seen. Along the northern border of Tennessee, buffalo trails (or traces) provided pathways for the explorers and early settlers.

De Soto's party in 1540 probably followed Indian trails from the upper Hiwassee River Valley to the site of Chattanooga, where there were towns of the Cherokee and Creeks. No doubt, de Soto followed Indian trade routes from north Mississippi to the fourth Chickasaw Bluff and the main town of the Chickasaws. Marquette and Joliet visited the Chickasaws in 1673, followed by La Salle in 1682, but they followed the rivers and made little use of trails. Dr. Thomas Walker's party is said to have been the first group of white men to find Cumberland Gap, but this important pass had been used by Indian raiders and traders for centuries. Gabriel Arthur accompanied a party of Cherokees through the gap in 1673. Daniel Boone, John Finley, and four others traveled from the Yadkin Valley in North Carolina through Cumberland Gap in 1769, following buffalo traces and Indian trails.

Daniel Boone's reports of the land beyond the great mountain barrier influenced a migration from the Yadkin Valley to Kentucky in 1773. The stream of settlers through the Cumberland Gap grew in spite of hostile Indians and white highwaymen who preyed on travelers. This route became known as the Wilderness Road.

Trails connected the Overhill Cherokee towns of Chota, Tallassee, and Tellico with the Hiwassee settlements and a trade route to South Carolina and the south Atlantic coast. The Black Fox Trail

1

ran from the Hiwassee settlements past a salt lick in the present Rhea County, past the Indian mounds east of Pikeville, and on across the Cumberland Plateau to the Caney Fork River.

In volume 1 of *Tennessee, The Volunteer State* (1923), John Trotwood Moore and Austin P. Foster tell of a branch of the Indian War Trail crossing Chilhowee Mountain at Millstone, Georgia, from Fort McTeer to the Cherokee town of Tuckaleechee. The Chickamauga Path began in the North Georgia and Chattanooga settlements, crossed the Tennessee River, and then crossed the Cumberland Plateau to Beersheba Springs. From there it went to the site of the present town of Rock Island, crossed the Caney Fork River, and passed a little west of the present town of Sparta, branching out at a fortified town on Cherry Creek. One fork went to the settlements of the Cherokees at Officer's Mounds near Algood and then to Carthage on the Cumberland River. The other fork went to the present site of Mayland and on beyond Jamestown. An important trail ran between the present towns of Monterey and Sparta, connected with the Chickamauga Path near the junction of the Cumberland, White, and Putnam county lines in the present community of Yankeetown. Settlers used this trail to move into the Calfkiller River Valley.

North of the Cumberland River, buffalo paths connected salt licks and provided trails for the settlers who moved from upper East Tennessee to French Lick, now Nashville. The buffalo disappeared from Middle and East Tennessee around the end of the seventeenth century, apparently because of excess hunting and, possibly, the rapid conversion to farmland of grassy uplands and rich bottomland forests and canebrakes. Natural changes in the habitat also may have been a factor.

The Natchez Trace, which provided a return route for flatboaters to the Nashville area, began as the Chickasaw Path of Peace. The Natchez Trace Parkway follows the general route of this historic trail. The Chickasaw Trace, mentioned by several historians, ran from the Chickasaw Bluffs eastward and seems to have crossed Tennessee near the mouth of Duck River. Another Chickasaw trail, the Massac Trace, passed through Madison County and College Street in Jackson. Other trails in Middle Tennessee, possibly used by Indians from Illinois seeking salt, ran from the salt licks north and west toward the Red River.

Captain James Robertson led a party overland from the Holston Country to French Lick in 1779, following buffalo paths from the Wilderness Road at Cumberland Gap westward through the Kentucky Country and down the Cumberland River to their destination. Meanwhile, the Donelson Party floated down the Holston and the Tennessee to the Ohio, then pushed back up the Cumberland River. The river trip to French Lick was the more hazardous, running through Chickamauga territory and through treacherous eddies and rapids. The settlement's name was changed from French Lick to Nashborough, and later to Nashville.

With the surge to settle the country west of the Appalachians, road building was emphasized. On November 6, 1786, Colonel Robertson was empowered to enlist 201 men to protect the inhabitants of the Nashville settlement and to cut a road from the Clinch River to Nashville. This clearing work began in August of 1787 at Clinch Mountain and proceeded along the route of an old Indian trail up Crooked Fork and Emory River, across the Cumberland Plateau and Highland Rim to the Cumberland River at Flynn's Creek and on to Nashville by September 1788. This North Carolina Military Trace, with periodic route and name changes, served as the main road across the Cumberlands to Nashville until 1802. In that year the Cumberland Turnpike Company opened a road along a more southerly route from Southwest Point (Kingston) through Crab Orchard and on to William Walton's ferry on the Cumberland near the mouth of the Caney Fork. Commonly known as the Walton Road, it soon became a major route westward from the Carolinas, Virginia, and Pennsylvania.

Around 1787 Glover's Trace ran across the Tennessee River into West Tennessee, down the valley of Trace Creek (today crossed several times by U.S. 70 in Humphreys County), then turned south through Henderson and McNairy counties into North Mississippi, with a branch extending to the Chickasaw Bluffs. John F. Brevard advocated opening the Glover's Trace for boatmen returning from New Orleans. Brevard's interest in opening Glover's Trace may have resulted from the activities of highwaymen who waylaid travelers on the Natchez Trace, robbing them of the proceeds from the sale of their goods and boats in New Orleans. Travelers on the Wilderness Road through Cumberland Gap suffered similar indignities. William Cocke arranged with the Chickasaws in 1815 to open Glover's Trace, but the government refused to bear any of the expense.

The early trails in Middle Tennessee, which generally followed the buffalo trails, were blazed according to the use for which they were suitable. One chop meant a footpath, two chops a packhorse route, and three chops indicated a wagon road. Roads were developed more slowly west of Nashville, probably because the commercial traffic followed the river.

The Tennessee Territory, ceded to the government by North Carolina in 1790, became a state in 1796. By 1804 county courts were permitted to build roads and to establish ferries. By a series of treaties between 1791 and 1819, the Cherokees relinquished all their lands except in the southeast corner of Tennessee. The Chickasaw territory in West Tennessee was purchased in 1818. The development of a young state called for mass means of moving goods and raw materials, and again an emphasis was placed on road building. Many of the old Indian trails became wagon roads, and eventually, the fast highways of today.

In Northwest Tennessee David Crockett used a few remaining trails to hunt bear and deer. Old Indian trails remained in use in the Great Smoky Mountains, and some of them are still in use in the national park as recreation trails. Today, it appears that U.S. 11W follows the Great Indian Warpath from Bristol and Kingsport down the Holston Valley to Knoxville. U.S. 25E follows a pioneer route from Bean Gap through Cumberland Gap. Some early migrants turned down the Powell Valley, following trails that have become Tenn. 63. U.S. 127 follows the Chickamauga Warpath through the Sequatchie Valley. U.S. 41 and I-24 follow the general route of the Nickajack Trace. U.S. 70S traces part of the Chickamauga Path between McMinnville and Sparta, while Tenn. 84 from Sparta to Monterey follows the Calfkiller River Route described earlier. Tenn. 30 follows the Black Fox Trail. The Natchez Trace has become a national parkway. U.S. 70 follows the old Glover's Trace westward from Nashville to the Tennessee River, while U.S. 64 probably takes the Chickasaw Route from Bolivar to Memphis.

The evolution from trail to wagon road to stagecoach road to automobile highway, along with the advent of the steamboat and the railroad, changed the travel habits of Tennesseans. Game trails remained along the ridges; cattle drovers used a few trails in the Smokies; hunters still roamed the mountains. The most famous hiker of the nineteenth century, John Muir, mostly followed roads, not trails, while crossing Tennessee from Jamestown to the Hiwassee River on his 1,000-mile walk to the Gulf. A new generation in a new era has revived interest in foot trails, however, and that interest means development and expansion of the trails system in Tennessee.

2. Trail Development in the Twentieth Century

At the turn of the century, a few old Indian trails still existed in the Appalachian Mountains, but the Great Warpath and the Indian trade routes had become wagon roads. Hunters used game trails along the crests of the ridges in the Cumberlands; footpaths existed along most of the rivers. Well-defined trails in the Smokies were used by cattlemen who pastured their stock on the high balds in the summertime. The cattle were driven up the mountain in spring and were brought back to lower elevations before the first snowfall. Logging companies built railroads into the mountains, and these were used by the few hunters and fishermen who had time for those pursuits. Few people went pleasure hiking.

The advent of the Boy Scout movement in 1910, with its emphasis on outdoor skills, including trail marking and hiking, brought a new interest in trails. It was still several years, however, before there was much trail development in Tennessee.

A growing interest in forest conservation influenced the Tennessee General Assembly to pass an enabling act in April 1901 permitting the federal government to purchase land in East Tennessee to establish public forest reservations. After more than forty attempts were made in Congress to pass a forest purchase law, Rep. John Weeks of Massachusetts introduced a successful bill in 1909; it was signed by President William Howard Taft in March 1911. Within two months of the signing of the Weeks Bill, several purchase units were established in Tennessee. Acquisition of private land started immediately. From 1911 to 1936 there were many changes in purchase units and forest boundaries; in 1936 President Franklin D. Roosevelt established the present Cherokee National Forest.

At the time of acquisition, only a few tracts of land were served by permanent road and trail facilities. One of the first jobs of the

U.S. Forest Service was to improve access. Trails were a means of getting materials into the mountains for building fire towers and inventorying the newly acquired timber resources. The first trail signs were installed on the Appalachian Trail in 1929 and the first trail guide pamphlets were issued in 1930, but little trail development occurred until the Civilian Conservation Corps (CCC) was created in 1933.

In the early twenties a group of influential citizens organized the Great Smoky Mountains Conservation Association for the purpose of getting a national park in the Smokies. Dr. Hubert Work, Secretary of the Interior under presidents Harding and Coolidge, had appointed a committee to study national park possibilities in the Southeast. This committee met with the association at the Mountain View Hotel in Gatlinburg on August 6, 1924. Paul Adams and Paul Fink, twentieth-century mountain men from Tennessee, told the group that the most spectacular area in the Southeast centered on Mount Le Conte. The next day Adams, Fink, and Wiley Oakley, a mountain man from Gatlinburg, led the group on a trip to Mount Le Conte. In order to pursue their campaign, the Great Smoky Mountains Conservation Association employed Paul Adams to establish a camp on top of Mount Le Conte. All materials except trees cut on the site were packed in on foot. The camp was started July 13, 1925, and later replaced by Mount Le Conte Lodge, which is still operating. The story of the camp is told in Paul Adams's *Mt. LeConte,* last printed in 1978. Adams is now deceased.

According to its fiftieth-anniversary handbook, a newly formed Smoky Mountains Hiking Club organized in 1924 joined the Appalachian Trail Conference in 1928 and pledged to sponsor construction of the Appalachian Trail through the proposed national park. The Great Smoky Mountains National Park became a reality in 1937, with assistance from the Rockefeller Foundation; many miles of trail have been built since then, adding up to a total of some 900 miles. Many good guides are available on the Smokies and the AT.

The Civilian Conservation Corps, created by the Franklin D.

Roosevelt administration during the Great Depression, built many miles of trails in state forests, national forests, the new national park, and in the Tennessee Valley Authority's demonstration parks around the new Norris Reservoir. Those parks—Norris Dam, Big Ridge, and Cove Lake—are now a part of Tennessee's State Park System. With the forty-hour workweek spawned by the depression, the people who were lucky enough to be employed found themselves with time to spare. Some of them found their way to the new trails built by the CCC. World War II interrupted nonessential public works, but the recreation boom continued to grow.

In 1958 Congress created the Outdoor Recreation Resources Review Commission (ORRRC) in an effort to determine future recreation needs. In 1962 the ORRRC reported that driving for pleasure was the primary recreational pursuit of the American public and that walking for pleasure ranked second. An updated study in 1967 showed that walking for pleasure had moved into first place. The Tennessee Department of Conservation's Division of State Parks published an inventory of the state's recreation resources in 1962. That report mentioned vacation trails in Standing Stone State Park and only nature trails in others. Only four parks had naturalist–nature trail programs. The Tennessee Outdoor Recreation Areas System (TORAS) plan now includes trails in at least fifty areas.

In March 1965 the Clinch and Powell River Valley Association (CPRVA) proposed the Cumberland Trail, to follow the crest of Cumberland Mountain from Cumberland Gap to Cove Lake State Park, then Walden Ridge to Oliver Springs, with a connecting trail to Oak Ridge. After a news release in area newspapers, CPRVA received fifteen letters offering help and permission to cross private land. A student intern from the Department of Political Science at the University of Tennessee explored land ownership on the proposed route that summer. But the association changed officers in July 1965, and the project fell by the wayside.

Tennessee Trails Association (TTA) was organized in November and December 1968, and the Cumberland Trail was chosen as a pilot project to prove the feasibility of a statewide trail system. The proposed route was extended to follow the highest ridges of the Cumberland Mountains to the Tennessee-Georgia state line. (Robert M. Howes, retired director of the Land Between the Lakes National Recreation Area, later informed the author that he had proposed such a trail when he was president of the Smoky Mountains Hiking Club.) TTA and the Department of Conservation sponsored the first state trail symposium at Montgomery Bell State Park, April 11, 1970. State and national agencies and a number of private organizations attended the meeting, and Rep. Robert Bible of the Tennessee General Assembly discussed a proposed state trails system act. It was decided that the TTA would work with Rep. Bible to refine the act for introduction in the 1971 session of the legislature. The Trails System Act, passed and signed by Governor Winfield Dunn in April 1971, designated seven state scenic trails and provided for recreation trails and side, or connecting, trails. The scenic trails were to be primarily foot trails, with provision for some bicycle and horse trails. Tennessee's was the first state trails system act.

An assistant commissioner in the Department of Conservation was responsible for scenic rivers, natural areas, and trails, all under a single administrator, and state parks. Joe Gaines, a forester who had been working as a state park naturalist, became the first state trails system administrator on March 1, 1972. Very little money was available at first, but nine new positions for trails and scenic rivers were approved by the Department of Personnel late in 1973. Supervisors for the Chickasaw Bluffs, Cumberland, and Lonesome Pine trails were employed at the beginning of 1974. Limited funds were budgeted for 1975, and master plans were prepared for the three trails. The Dunn administration asked for $600,000 for trails in the 1976 budget. But Ray Blanton, governor for the term beginning January 1975, impounded the remaining funds in the 1975 budget and withdrew the $600,000 Dunn request.

The Conservation Department had not officially recognized the sections of the Cumberland Trail built by the Tennessee Trails Association, so in 1976 the TTA became a nonprofit corporation to provide a legal entity for agreements with landowners and to maintain continuity of the scenic trails program. Work continued on the southern end of the Cumberland Trail on public land. The efforts of the state trails system staff were diverted to state parks and to the new South Cumberland Recreation Complex, which includes Grundy Forest, Stone Door, and Savage Gulf State Natural Areas, some TVA land, and private lands in Grundy and Marion counties. The complex is a joint effort by TVA, the state of Tennessee, and the local development district.

TTA's South Cumberland Trail Committee was organized on December 12, 1972, at Signal Mountain. Under the leadership of chairman Sam Powell, the committee, in cooperation with the Division of Forestry and Cumberland Trail coordinator David Shupe, had completed 10 miles of trail from Signal Point to Prentice Cooper State Forest by early 1978.

The trails program was accelerated in state parks and recreation areas in 1976 and 1977. Administrator Gaines reported to the Tennessee Trails Association's annual meeting on November 19, 1977, that more than 200 miles of trail had been constructed during the preceding two years. The trails program received a boost during the 1977 Tennessee legislative session when House Bill 199 was passed, authorizing the Commissioner of Conservation to enter into agreements with nonprofit corporations with regard to recreational and natural areas and facilities, to provide park rangers for such publicly and privately owned areas used by the general public, and to acquire lands adjacent to such areas. Tennessee already had a landowners' liability law, passed in 1963, opening more land for hunting, fishing, and other outdoor recreation. TTA used this law successfully in getting permission to build trails across private land. This law also influenced Bowater Southern Paper Corporation to open its lands for public recreation and to initiate a pocket wilderness program, described in chapter 11.

The Conservation Department found some extra money in 1977 and launched a cooperative program with TTA to implement sections of the Cumberland Trail and the Trail of the Lonesome

Pine. Mrs. Floy Bostic was employed to contact landowners along the latter route, with trail chairman Gordon Newland of Kingsport coordinating her efforts. They knew the people of the area and were highly successful in getting permission to build the trail across private property. David Shupe worked with TTA on a 22-mile stretch on the north end of the Cumberland Trail. A large industrial landowner, the American Association, gave written permission to develop the trail across its land. The A. P. Huber Company, which acquired this property, has continued the agreement. Mr. and Mrs. Earl Hobson Smith, owners of McClain Rock, gave verbal permission. A Young Adult Conservation Corps (YACC) crew was assigned to this section in the fall of 1978.

The Big South Fork National River and Recreation Area, developed by the U.S. Army Corps of Engineers and managed by the National Park Service, has more than 200 miles of hiking trails and 130 miles of horse trails. It is located in Fentress, Pickett, Morgan, and Scott counties in Tennessee and McCreary County in Kentucky. The Sheltowee Trace National Recreation Trail has been extended into Pickett County to connect with the John Muir State Scenic Trail, which passes through the Big South Fork. TVA provided labor to help build trails, which were planned by a private contractor for the Corps of Engineers.

During the Carter administration, TVA used YACC labor to build trails on its reservoir properties and to assist state and county agencies with their trail programs, as well as the Big South Fork Project. More recently, labor from the Regional State Prison in Morgan County has been used for trail work. During the 1970s, TVA and the state of Tennessee cooperated in an attempt to convert abandoned railroad beds to trails for hiking, bicycling, and horseback riding. As a result of disputes over land ownership and resentment of abuses by motorcycle riders, the program has been dropped for the time being.

There has been strong interest in trails on the local level also. The North Ridge Trail in Oak Ridge was built by Tennessee Citizens for Wilderness Planning (TCWP). It was designated a National

Recreational Trail in 1973, the first within a city to be so named. TCWP still maintains the trail, with the assistance of local scout troops. The Department of Conservation, City of Murfreesboro, Middle Tennessee State University, and Rutherford County cooperated in establishing the Rutherford County Bicycle Touring System in 1975. This was followed by the development of a hiking-horseback-canoe system in 1977 on lands of the Corps of Engineers J. Percy Priest project. The Corps has developed other trails on its projects, some with the assistance of TTA volunteers and scout troops.

Governor Lamar Alexander, who was inaugurated in 1979, supported the trail system and set 1985 as the goal for completion of the Cumberland Trail. TTA established an "Adopt-a-Trail" program in 1982, and its members and chapters are maintaining a number of trails. Other organizations have joined the movement, and TCWP maintains the Whites Creek Trail on TVA land and property on Watts Bar Lake. The Sierra Club has adopted several trails.

Holdouts used the threat of condemnation to stir resentment among landowners on Clinch Mountain, and the state backed off the Trail of the Lonesome Pine in 1984. The administration of Governor Ned Ray McWherter, faced with budget problems, gave trails a low priority in 1987, and new trail construction came to a halt. The state trails system administrator position was abolished in 1988.

In 1990 as part of the McWherter administration's 10 percent budget cut for all departments of state government, the Department of Environment and Conservation completely eliminated operating funds for the Cumberland State Scenic Trail. Since that time no maintenance work has been done on C.T. Sections one, two, and three, and a few of the private landowners have even posted the trail crossing on their property. For now, therefore, these sections are effectively closed to through-hikers.

There are still good relations between the Department of Environment and Conservation and the TTA, and volunteer work continues. Standards have been set for trail maintenance, and work continues at all levels. Several state parks have been added since 1971, and each has a trail system.

Passage of the State and Local Parks Partnership Act of 1990 by the Tennessee General Assembly and of the Symms National Recreational Trails Fund Act of 1991 by the U.S. Congress promise a reinvigoration of trail improvement and expansion throughout Tennessee at all levels of government and the private sector. Pursuant to the Symm's Act, a Tennessee Recreation Trails Advisory Board was created by the Department of Environment and Conservation; the board held its first meeting May 24, 1993.

3. Cherokee National Forest

Cherokee National Forest extends along the eastern border of Tennessee from the Virginia line on the north to Great Smoky Mountains National Park, then from the southern end of the park to the Georgia line. It is surrounded by other national forests in the neighboring states: Jefferson in Virginia, Pisgah and Nantahala in North Carolina, and Chattahoochee in Georgia. It is divided into six ranger districts, three on each side of the national park. Federal ownership is not continuous within the designated boundaries of the forest. The north end has the greater percentage of its area in private ownership. The Tellico and Ocoee ranger districts in the south end have the most land in public ownership. From the northeast to the southwest, the ranger districts are Watauga, Unaka, Nolichucky, Tellico, Hiwassee, and Ocoee. These were the homelands of the Cherokee Indians, traversed by the rivers that head the Tennessee Valley—the Holston, Watauga, Nolichucky, Little Tennessee, Tellico, Hiwassee, and Ocoee.

While no up-to-date maps of the trail system in the Cherokee National Forest are now available, one is to be published soon. For trail information write Cherokee National Forest, P.O. Box 2010, Cleveland, TN 37320.

Watauga Ranger District

Headquarters are located at Route 9, Box 2235, Elizabethton, TN 37643. This district has a total of 110.5 mi. in ten trails, including the Appalachian Trail. We describe two trails: an 8-mi. section of the Holston Mountain Trail and the Iron Mountain Trail. Most of the others are in various stages of neglect or interference by other forest uses, according to district personnel.

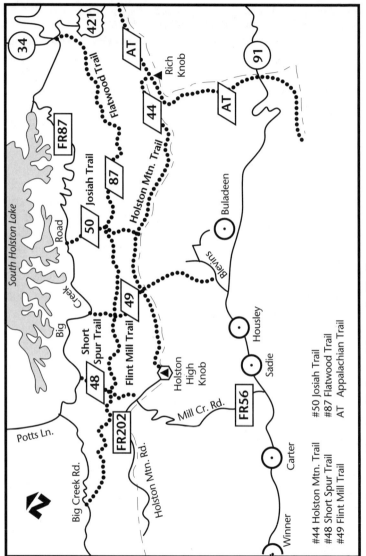

Watauga Ranger District, Holston Mountain Trail

#44 Holston Mtn. Trail   #50 Josiah Trail
#48 Short Spur Trail   #87 Flatwood Trail
#49 Flint Mill Trail   AT   Appalachian Trail

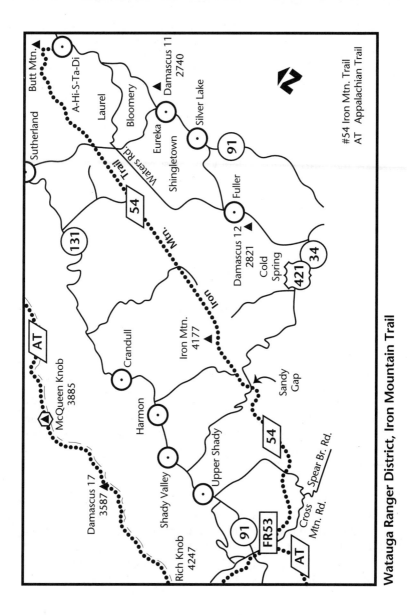

#54 Iron Mtn. Trail
AT Appalachian Trail

Watauga Ranger District, Iron Mountain Trail

Holston Mountain Trail. Number 44, Carter, Doe, and Shady Valley, USGS quads 207 NE, 214 NW, 213 SW. Length, 8.29 mi. plus road hike of 1 mi.; rating, difficult. From Elizabethton go northeast on Tenn. 91 for about 1.5 mi. past Carter to Panhandle Road (Forest Service Road FR 56) and turn left. Go 4.2 mil. on FR 56 to fork on crest of Holston Mountain. Turn right on FR 56A and go 0.2 mi. to gate with roadside parking. Walk 1 mi. on FR 56A past gate to Holston High Knob lookout tower, elevation 4,100 ft. The trail runs northeast along the crest of Holston Mountain to Flint Mill Trail, number 49. There are views of South Holston Lake to the west and of the Iron Mountains to the east. The trail swings north and continues along the crest about 4 mi. to the Josiah Trail (3,500 ft.), climbs gradually to the Carter-Sullivan county line (3,700 ft.), and follows the ridgetop to the junction with the Appalachian Trail on Rich Knob at 4,247 ft. Double Springs trail shelter is at this junction.

A possible loop hike starts from Holston High Knob, turns left on the Flint Mill Trail, and drops down the mountain to Flat Woods Horse Trail, number 87. Turn left on the Flat Woods Trail to Short Spur Trail, number 48; go left to FR 202; then left again to Holston High Knob—total distance, 8 to 9 mi. Clockwise: leave car at junction of FR 202 and Short Spur Trail and start down the mountain from there.

Iron Mountain Trail. Number 54, Shady Valley and Laurel Bloomery USGS quads, 213SW and 213SE. Length, 16.97 mi.; rating, difficult. From Elizabethton, take TN-91 northeast 20 mi. to the top of Cross Mountain. Turn right on Cross Mountain Road (FR 53) and go 1.5 mi. to the top of Iron Mountain and the trailhead. The elevation at the start is about 3,700 ft. The trail runs east and northeast on the crest of Iron Mountain, 4,000 ft. elevation, with views of Shady Valley and Holston Mountain to the west and Laurel Creek Valley and the mountains along the North Carolina line on the east. It follows the crest at an average elevation of 3,900 ft., crossing Sandy Gap and U.S. 421 at 3,862 ft. From Sandy Gap the trail curves northward, then heads northwest about a mile to FR 234; continuing along the crest of the Iron Mountains, it gradually descends to 3,500 ft. at Morfield Ridge. The trail continues northeast at about 3,500 ft., curves right, and drops down Butt Mountain to the vicinity of Laurel Creek and Tenn. 91 in the center of Camp A-Hi-S-Ta-Di, a Methodist Church camp north of Laurel Bloomery and near the Virginia line. Since this trail follows the crest of the mountain, it may be necessary to drop down the mountainside to find water. Parking at the FR 53 trailhead is limited and on private land, but good parking is available at Sandy Gap and Camp A-Hi-S-Ta-Di.

Unaka Ranger District

The ranger station is located at 1205 North Main Street, Erwin, TN 37650. We have chosen what appear to be the three best foot trails. All are on the Unicoi USGS quad, 199NE.

Patty Ridge Trail. Number 113. Length, 2.6 mi.; rating, difficult in the upper reaches. Follow Tenn. 81 south from Jonesboro and turn right on FR 136 past Embreeville to the confluence of Patty's Creek and the Nolichucky River. No parking is provided at the trailhead. This trail is a favorite of hunters in season. It goes up Patty Creek to about 1,800 ft. elevation and veers left, climbing to 2,200 ft. in 0.5 mi. It ascends a gentle slope across a ridge, 2,300 ft. maximum elevation, then drops off to Broad Shoal Creek at about 1,900 ft. The Patty's Ridge wildlife food plot is at milepost 2.6. The trail turns right along the ridge and ends at the Rich Mountain hunter access road. This trail provides a good spring flower walk, with the added pleasure of mountain streams.

Limestone Cove Trail. Number 30. Length, 3.2 mi.; rating, difficult. This is one of two foot trails in the Unaka Mountain Wilderness and has two trailheads. The lower trailhead is 4 mi. east of Unicoi off Tenn. 107 at the Limestone Cove Recreation Area. Park at the recreation area, elevation 2,100 ft., and follow FR 4343 to Rocky Branch, 2,600 ft. It becomes steeper briefly, then levels off

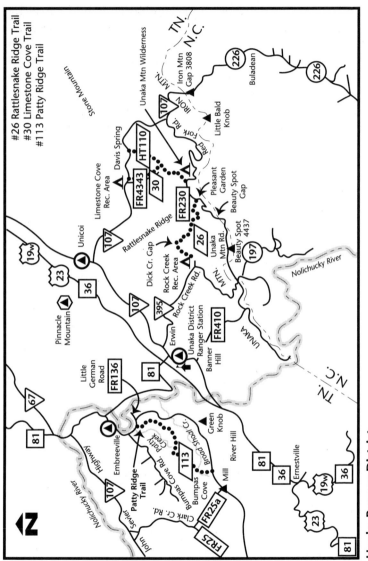

#26 Rattlesnake Ridge Trail
#30 Limestone Cove Trail
#113 Patty Ridge Trail

Unaka Ranger District

slightly on an easier climb to 2,800 ft. It follows an old logging road to the top of Stamping Ground Ridge, crosses the head of a branch at 4,300 ft., and curves left at 4,500 ft. There is an easy slope for 0.5 mi., on which this trail coincides with trail number 110, which is a horseback-riding trail. The Limestone Cove Trail ends at Unaka Mountain Road, FR 230, which provides an easy southwest climb to the Unaka Mountain Overlook and Pleasant Garden, elevation 4,800 ft. The second of the Unaka Mountain Wilderness foot trails begins on the west side of the overlook parking lot.

Rattlesnake Ridge Trail. Number 26. Length, 3.59 mi.; rating, moderately difficult. From Unaka district office go 3 mi. to Rock Creek Recreation Area by TN-395; or continue another 2 mi. to Indian Grave Gap (North Carolina–Tennessee state line) on TN-395, turn left on FR-230, and go approximately 6 mi. to Unaka Mountain Overlook. The trail drops from elevation 4,840 ft. at Unaka Overlook to 2,100 ft. at Rock Creek Recreation Area. It provides views of Beauty Spot in the upper portion and passes through several forest types (cove hardwoods, upland hardwoods, table mountain pine, and white pine–hemlock). It follows Rattlesnake Ridge to Dick Creek Gap, then Rattlesnake Creek to Rock Creek.

Nolichucky Ranger District

Office is located at 120 Austin Avenue, Greeneville, TN 37743. We find twenty-six trails listed on the trail map, sixteen of which are designated as hiking trails. Two of the horseback trails are of such scenic value that we also recommend them to hikers. Hikers are asked to step well back from the trail when a rider passes, to keep from spooking the horse. We complained of vandalism in our first edition, but the district ranger writes that the Nolichucky has no worse vandalism problem than other districts or other public lands. The Squibb Creek Trail, number 23, the link between the Horse Creek Recreation Area and the Appalachian Trail, now ends at the Forest Service boundary. We have not described any of the

#13 Greene Mountain Trail

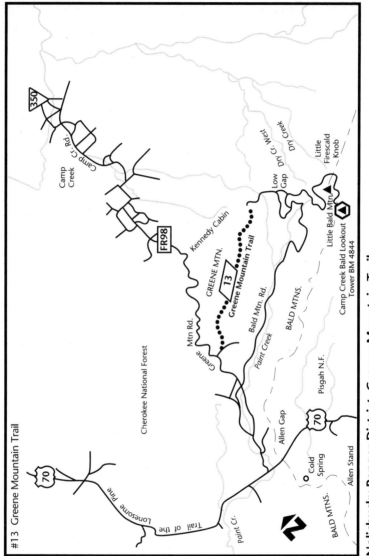

Nolichucky Ranger District, Greene Mountain Trail

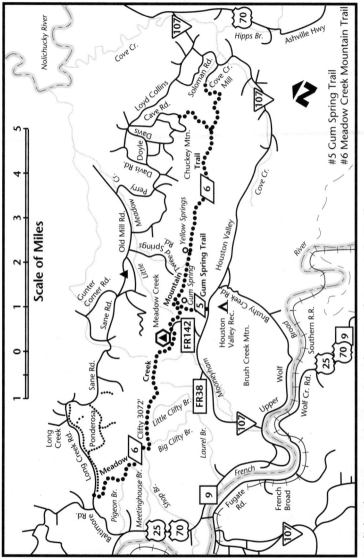

Nolichucky Ranger District, Meadow Creek Mountain Trail

#5 Gum Spring Trail
#6 Meadow Creek Mountain Trail

Scale of Miles

AT because of the numerous other guidebooks covering it. We describe three trails in the district.

Greene Mountain Trail. Number 13. USGS quad sheets Greystone, 190SW, and Lake Davy Crockett, 181SE. Length, 3.6 mi.; rating, moderate. This trail has been designated for horseback and hiking use. To get there take Greene Mountain Road, FR 98, either from the Camp Creek community south of Greeneville, or north from U.S. 70 near Allen Gap on the Tennessee–North Carolina line. The trail starts from FR 98 at a wide curve on the crest of Greene Mountain, where an abandoned timber road leads off to the west. It starts up the ridge on a sharp slope, turns right at 2,500 ft. elevation after about 200 yds., and climbs to 3,700 ft. There is an easy slope for 0.5 mi. to 3,800 ft., then a mile along the crest of the mountain at an average elevation of 3,900 ft. Then the trail doubles back and runs south to end at Kennedy Cabin Road, which intersects Bald Mountain Road about 1.5 mi. down the south side of the mountain. There are views of the Bald Mountains to the south, the high peaks of the Smokies to the southeast, and the Nolichucky River Valley to the north.

Meadow Creek Mountain Trail. Number 6. USGS quad sheets Lake Davy Crockett, 181SE, and Paint Rock, 182NW. Length, about 14 mi.; rating, moderate. Access to this trail is available at four locations: from U.S. 25-70 via Baltimore Road and Long Creek Road, about 10 mi. east of Newport; via FR 142, Meadow Creek Lookout Tower Road, off Tenn. 107, about 4 mi. northeast of U.S. 25-70; via Gum Spring Trail, number 5, from Holston Valley Recreation Area on Tenn. 107; or from Tenn. 107-70 at Cove Creek, 10 mi. south of Greeneville.

Starting from the east end, at the Cove Creek crossing, elevation 1,380 ft., the trail follows the creek upstream 0.5 mi. to 1,600 ft., curves left, and climbs the ridge to 2,000 ft. It curves sharply left and angles up the mountainside to the crest of Chuckey Mountain, elevation 2,300 ft., switches back, and climbs to the top of the ridge over a low peak at 2,650 ft. The trail follows the crest of the mountain southwest, up and down, to arrive at a saddle and the junction with Gum Springs Trail at 2,500 ft. An old telephone pole with an insulator and scrap of wire marks this intersection. There is water a short distance down Gum Springs Trail to the left. The trail crosses the saddle onto Meadow Creek Mountain and climbs to 2,700 ft., continuing along the crest to Meadow Creek Tower Road. Crossing the road, the trail runs west 0.5 mi. to a microwave tower and the Meadow Creek lookout tower at 2,875 ft. From the tower the trail follows the mountain southwest about 2 mi., then begins the climb to Clifty, elevation 3,072 ft. It curves west and drops to 2,400 ft. in 0.5 mi. Following the contour briefly, it drops sharply 200 ft., then slopes easily down to 2,000 ft. Here the trail descends the side of the ridge to 1,600 ft., crosses a low ridge, and drops down to Long Creek at 1,300 ft. U.S. 25-70 is 1.5 mi. down the creek. This trail has been opened to horseback use.

Gum Springs Trail. Number 5. Paint Rock USGS quad, 182 NW. Length, 1.3 mi.; rating, easy. This trail provides access to the Meadow Creek Mountain Trail, number 6, from the Holston Valley Recreation Area on Tenn. 107, about 5 mi. northeast of U.S. 25-70. The trailhead is directly across the highway from the entrance to the Holston Valley Recreation Area, which has good running water and a campground. The trail starts at about 1,800 ft. elevation and switches back onto an abandoned road at about 200 yds.; 100 yds. farther another road follows the hillside up a gentle slope. At 0.3 mi. it crosses the toe of the hill and follows downslope along a steep hillside on the right, crosses a ravine, and arrives at another abandoned road. It turns up the road to the right, crossing and recrossing the spring branch for about 1 mi. to the junction with the Meadow Creek Mountain Trail at 2,500 ft. elevation. An additional 1.3 mi. from the gap to Yellow Springs Road is not being maintained.

Tellico Ranger District

This district is a close second to the Watauga in the number of recreational visits among the six districts in Cherokee National Forest. It has the highest percentage of land in public ownership

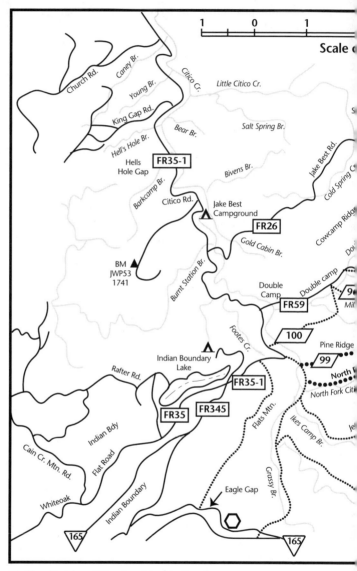

Tellico Ranger District, North Section

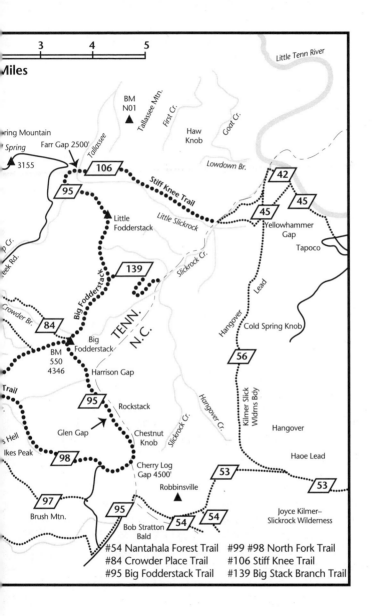

Miles

3   4   5

Little Tenn River

BM
N01
Tallassee Mtn.
First Cr.
Haw
Knob
Goat Cr.

ring Mountain
Spring
3155
Farr Gap 2500'
Tallassee
106
95
Little
Fodderstack
Big Fodderstack
Lowdown Br.
Stiff Knee Trail
Little Slickrock
139
Slickrock Cr.

42
45
45
Yellowhammer
Gap
Tapoco

Crowder Br.
84
BM
550
4346
Big
Fodderstack
TENN.
N.C.
Hangover Lead
Cold Spring Knob
56

Trail
95
Rockstack
Harrison Gap
Hangover Cr.
Slickrock Cr.
Kilmer Slick Wldrns Bdy
Hangover

s Hell
Ikes Peak
98
Glen Gap
Chestnut
Knob
Cherry Log
Gap 4500'
Robbinsville
53
53
Haoe Lead

97
Brush Mtn.
95
Bob Stratton
Bald
54
54
Joyce Kilmer–
Slickrock Wilderness

#54 Nantahala Forest Trail   #99 #98 North Fork Trail
#84 Crowder Place Trail   #106 Stiff Knee Trail
#95 Big Fodderstack Trail   #139 Big Stack Branch Trail

and the greatest number of hiking trails, thirty-three in all. Most of the trails are well maintained and get a lot of traffic. The district ranger office is located off Tellico River Road about 4 mi. east of Tellico Plains; the mailing address is Route 3, Tellico Plains, TN 37385. We describe only a few of the typical trails.

Many backpackers leave their cars at Tapoco, North Carolina, elevation 1,200 ft., on U.S. 129, and take Nantahala National Forest trail number 45 down the Little Tennessee River and up Ike Branch to Hangover Lead on the border of the Joyce Kilmer–Slickrock Wilderness. Going south to Yellowhammer Gap, a total distance of 2 mi. from the trailhead, turn west 0.5 mi. down to Slickrock Creek and the junction with Nantahala trail number 42, elevation 1,320 ft. It is 0.5 mi. up Slickrock Creek to the junction with Cherokee National Forest trail number 106 (Stiff Knee), elevation 1,400 ft., on the Tennessee–North Carolina state line. Stiff Knee Trail, rated moderate, leads up Little Slickrock Creek to Farr Gap and the start of Fodderstack Trail at 2,800 ft., a distance of 3.2 mi. Both trails are in the Citico Creek Wilderness.

Big Fodderstack Trail. Number 95. USGS quad sheet 140NE, Whiteoak Flats. Length, 10.4 mi.; rating, moderate. This trail is now listed for horseback and hiking use. To get to the Farr Gap trailhead parking area, take the Double Camp Road, FR 59, from the Indian Boundary Recreation Area, or Jake Best (Cold Spring) Road, FR 26, from Citico Road, FR 35-1. The parking area is at 2,720 ft. elevation. The trail starts on a short climb to the southwest past the junction with Stiff Knee Trail to the toe of a ridge at 3,000 ft., following an old road that has been closed to vehicular traffic. Open fields on the right offer excellent views of the surrounding mountains. The trail curves southward along the wilderness boundary, skirts the peak of Little Fodderstack Mountain, and continues to the junction of Crowder Creek Trail, number 84, 2.65 mi. from Farr Gap, and Big Stack Branch Trail, number 139, at an old farm called the Crowder Place. There are a spring and one of several campsites here, but don't trust the water.

From the Crowder Place the Big Fodderstack Trail follows the crest of the ridge at 3,500 ft. to Big Stack Gap, dropping slightly, then climbing back to 4,000 ft. elevation at the junction with trail number 99 on Big Fodderstack Mountain. This trail drops off the mountain to Citico Road. Big Fodderstack Trail turns sharply left and skirts the peak at about 4,200 ft., curves right, and drops to about 3,800 ft. at the state line. Running south by east, the trail climbs to 4,200 ft., skirts Rockstack Peak, passes through Glenn Gap, and crosses the top of Chestnut Knob, following the state line to the junction with the North Fork Trail, number 98, at Cherry Log Gap at about 4,500 ft. Big Fodderstack Trail continues along the state line ridge to an intersection with Nantahala Trail, number 54, near Bob Stratton Bald. From there the trail turns southwest and descends to Cold Springs Gap parking area at an elevation of 4,200 ft. Here the trail terminates. From the Crowder Place to Strawberry Knob, the tread is hand dug.

Trail 98, following the North Fork of Citico Creek, traverses a laurel thicket known as Jeffrey's Hell, named for the ordeal of a hunter who became lost while searching for a lost dog. Hikers may follow the state line from Cherry Log Gap to Bob Bald along trail number 95 and pick up Nantahala Forest trail number 54, Stratton Bald Trail, which leads to the Joyce Kilmer Memorial Forest. From Stratton Bald Trail number 53 leads along the crest between Joyce Kilmer and Slickrock to Haoe Lookout, from which number 56 leads to the Hangover and down Hangover Lead back to Yellowhammer Gap. There are several good trails off North River Road that can be made into day loops. The next trail is in the Bald River Wilderness.

Bald River Trail. Number 88. Bald River Falls USGS quad, 140SW. Length, 5.6 mi.; rating, easy. This is a popular trail for day hikes along a roaring mountain stream, but it also has some good streamside campsites. Bald River is a wild trout stream, restricted to fly fishing and requiring a special permit. The trail is easy enough that a hiker can make it both ways in a day; a car shuttle can be arranged, but it requires a 15-mi. trip across a mountain. The trail starts at the parking area on Tellico River Road, FR 210, at Bald River Falls. There is a 200-ft. climb on a paved switchback path to the pic-

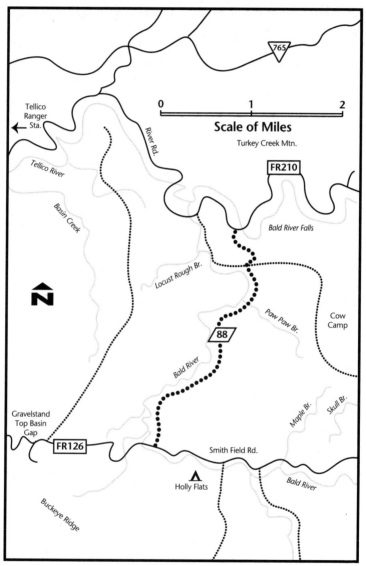

Tellico Ranger District, South Section

nic area above the falls. From the picnic area there is another steep climb to the top of a narrow gorge, a left turn on a rock outcropping, then a steep descent to a trail sloping down along the side of a cliff to a series of waterfalls. From here on the traffic diminishes.

As the trail levels out briefly, there is a rock house on the left, an overhanging rock that provides shelter from foul weather. This is the first trailside campsite. The trail follows an old logging railroad bed awhile, then rises to a narrow path along the side of the gorge, crosses a narrow ridge, and comes back to the railroad bed. This area was logged in the early part of the century before it became part of the national forest, and the logging company ran Sunday excursions from Tellico Plains to Bald River Falls. At about the halfway point there is another campsite at Pawpaw Branch. From here on the trail becomes easier, with vertical curves that break up the long slopes. The trail alternately follows the riverbank and rises away from the stream as the gorge narrows. The final campsite is at the turnaround for the old logging railroad. Bits of coal in the path mark this spot. At the final rise, laurel and rhododendron grow profusely along the path. A final 100-yd. descent ends under a huge rhododendron at Bald River Road. To the left is Holly Flats Recreation Area. The net elevation change is less than 500 ft. in 5 mi.

Hiwassee Ranger District

This district has two distinguishing features—the Hiwassee State Scenic River and the Gee Creek Wilderness, one of three in Cherokee National Forest that are part of the National Wilderness System. There has been no trail development in Gee Creek Wilderness, but visitors follow old abandoned roads and primitive footpaths. The district has only six foot trails, including the John Muir State Scenic Trail. The National Park Service's Bartram Trail Study eliminated the proposal for foot trails extending into the Hiwassee Ranger District.

John Muir Trail. Length, 18 mi.; rating, easy. This trail follows the route taken by John Muir on his 1,000-mile walk to the Gulf of

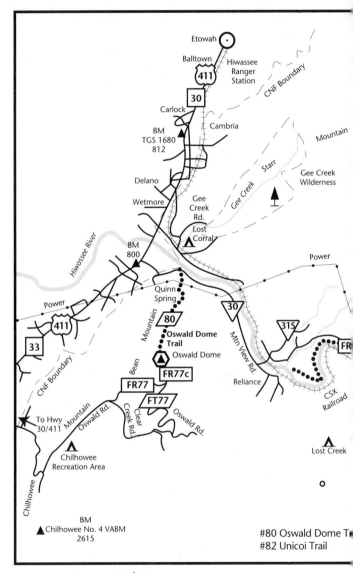

Hiwassee Ranger District

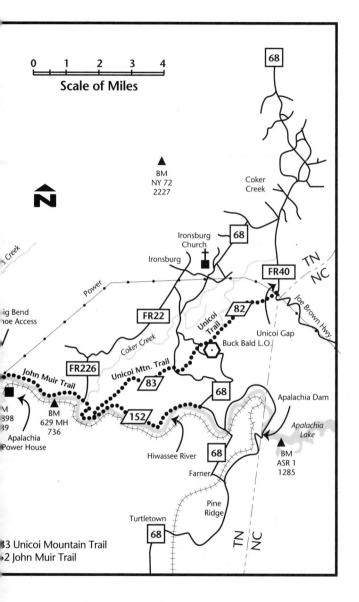

Scale of Miles
0 1 2 3 4

N

68

BM
NY 72
2227

Coker
Creek

Ironsburg
Church

68

Ironsburg

FR40

TN
NC

Power

82

Joe Brown Hwy.

FR22

Unicoi
Trail

Unicoi Gap

Big Bend
Canoe Access

Coker Creek

Buck Bald L.O.

John Muir Trail

FR226

Unicoi Mtn. Trail

83

68

Apalachia Dam

Apalachia
Lake

M
398
39

BM
629 MH
736

152

Apalachia
Power House

Hiwassee River

68

BM
ASR 1
1285

Farner

Pine
Ridge

Turtletown

68

TN
NC

33 Unicoi Mountain Trail
2 John Muir Trail

Mexico. It is a National Recreation Trail and is included in the State Scenic Trails System but was built by the U.S. Forest Service with YCC and YACC labor. To get to the trailhead, turn east off U.S. 411 on Tenn. 30, left across the bridge at Reliance, and right on the first road, FR 108, which leads 0.5 mi. to the trailhead at Childers Creek and on to canoe accesses along the river and to the Appalachia Power House. There is also access to the trail at several other points along this road. The trail follows the riverbank, an easy path along a beautiful stream, through lush vegetation with many wildflowers. It crosses the Big Bend canoe access 3.0 mi. upriver and parallels FR 108 and the river another 3 mi. to the swinging bridge at the powerhouse. The trail passes under the end of the bridge and continues on upriver to Tenn. 68. Near the end it climbs a rise about 200 ft., then drops back to an old road along the riverbank. Above the powerhouse the river becomes a trickle, as the water flows through a tunnel from Appalachia Dam.

Oswald Dome Trail. Number 80. Oswald Dome USGS quad, 126NE. Length, approximately 5 mi.; rating, moderate. The trail starts from Quinn Springs campground, 1.5 mi. east of U.S. 411 on Tenn. 30, elevation 750 ft. There is no water on the trail, so fill your canteen at Quinn Springs. The trail starts uphill in open woods, crosses a power line, and turns uphill to the right; turning left into open woods again, it gradually climbs to 1,040 ft. It switches back to the left at a ravine, curves left across a second ravine, then right around the toe of a hill. There is an easy ascent to the crest at 1,200 ft., where the trail levels out for the first time. It passes through a shallow saddle and up the crest of a hill to 1,400 ft. elevation, then curves left, winding along a rocky hillside on Bean Mountain. There is a continuous upgrade as the trail climbs the left side of the ridge, crossing the end of a hill and switching to the other side of the ridge.

Up the steep side of the ridge to the crest, the trail passes through a thicket into an open space that provides a view of the towns in the valley to the north. It switches back around the point of a ridge, continuing uphill. A pileated woodpecker sounds off nearby. Going southwest up a shallow valley between ridges, the trail arrives at the top of the ridge and switches back right up a moderate slope for 100 yds. It becomes steeper for 0.3 mi., a rocky path along the side of the crest. Topping a rise on Chilhowee Mountain, the trail levels out at about 3,000 ft. elevation in open woods, gently rolling terrain on a broad mountaintop strewn with boulders. A climb of about 0.5 mi. along the crest of a narrow ridge flattens out on top, and the mountain drops off steeply to the west. The trail drops into a saddle, then climbs uphill again to an old logging road. There is a gentle upgrade the last 0.8 mi., flattening out the final 100 yds. to arrive at Oswald Dome fire tower, elevation 3,500 ft. FR 77 leads from Oswald Dome to Chilhowee Recreation Area in the Ocoee Ranger District.

Unicoi Mountain Trail. Number 83. Farmer and McFarland USGS quads, 133NE and 133NW. Length, 6 mi.; rating, moderate. This trail runs from Tenn. 68 to the mouth of Coker Creek at FR 22. To get to the mouth of Coker Creek, turn west off Tenn. 68 on the road to Ironsburg Church, then left on FR 22. The trailhead on Tenn. 68 is 6.4 mi. south of the Coker Creek Post Office at a gap in Unicoi Mountain, elevation 1,700 ft. From there the trail follows an old logging road in a southwesterly direction 0.8 mi. and gradually rises to 2,000 ft. in the first 1.3 mi.; it follows the crest about a mile at this elevation. A ruffed grouse walks into the trail ahead, fluffs its ruff, and bobs its tail nervously, then flies. The trail swings gradually to the west, then curves south and drops off the toe of the ridge to about 1,400 ft. There is a slight rise over a hill before it veers right to follow a long slope back to 1,400 ft. Left down a ridge to 1,200 ft., it crosses another hill and drops to the Hiwassee River at about 950 ft. elevation.

Unicoi Trail. Number 82. Farmer USGS quad, 133NE. Length, 4.5 mi.; rating, moderate. This trail runs from Tenn. 68 south of the Unicoi Mountain Trail to Unicoi Gap on the state line. A gravel road known as the Joe Brown Highway crosses the historic gap 3 mi. from the Coker Creek Post Office and continues through Nantahala National Forest.

This trail is marked as a motorcycle trail from Tenn. 68 to Unicoi Gap. Starting at 1,700 ft. elevation, the trail follows an old roadbed in a steady climb along the side of the mountain about a mile to the junction mentioned above, at 2,200 ft. Buck Bald fire tower is above on the right, at 2,348 ft., but heavy timber hides the tower from view on the contour of this hill. The trail follows the crest of Unicoi Mountain at an average elevation of 2,000 ft., rises over a peak near the end, and drops off to cross a power line, then heads downhill to Unicoi Gap. Most of the trail runs through open woods inhabited by deer, squirrels, ruffed grouse, wild turkeys, and a host of songbirds.

Ocoee Ranger District

The office is 3 mi. east of Parksville on U.S. 64. The mailing address is Route 1 Parksville, Benton, TN 37307. The Ocoee Ranger District of Cherokee National Forest lies entirely within Polk County in the southeastern corner of Tennessee. U.S. 64 provides easy access from Chattanooga and Cleveland. The recreation pressure along this corridor exceeds that of the Tellico District. Parksville Lake at the western entrance and the Ocoee River above this impoundment attract many boaters, fishermen, and white-water enthusiasts. A number of outfitters provide raft trips on the most exciting white-water stream in the state, rivaling the Chattooga in Georgia and the Nantahala in North Carolina. In spite of the heavy traffic along the Ocoee River and the popularity of recreation areas north of U.S. 64, much of the section south of the river remains remote and wild.

The Cohutta Wilderness spills over from the Chattahoochee into the Ocoee District, and the Big Frog Wilderness adjoins this. The Cherokee National Forest trail map lists twenty-two foot trails, most of which have received maintenance since 1986. There is a problem with vandalism of signs, and the trails may not be well marked, so the hiker should have a map before venturing into the remote areas. Many of the trails are blazed in white, but the USFS is in the process of removing paint blazes in all wildernesses. We describe an outstanding loop bordering Cohutta Wilderness and the Chestnut Mountain Trail, which provides access to the wilderness.

Wolf Ridge, Big Frog, Grassy Gap, Big Creek Trails. Total length of loop, 9.5 mi.; rating, difficult. To get there turn south off of U.S. 64, 0.5 mi. west of the Ocoee River Bridge, onto the Cookson Creek Road. Proceed 2.8 mi. to the sign for Cookson Creek Church and continue straight ahead on Baker Creek Road, FR 55, 8.4 mi. to site of former Sheeds Creek Checking Station; turn left off FR 221, go 4.1 mi. to FR 221E, turn right, and travel 0.3 mi. to the trailhead. Because of the long grades and rough areas, travel time is included in this description. There is almost continuous upgrade the first 4 mi.

Beginning at Pace Gap, elevation 1,654 ft., Wolf Ridge Trail, number 66, runs generally south about a mile, ascending the ridge to 2,300 ft. It bears right, crosses Bear Pen Hill at 2,640 ft., and drops into Grassy Gap at 2,500 ft. Hiking time so far is thirty-five minutes. Staying to the right at the junction with the Grassy Gap Trail, continue up the crest another twenty minutes to the junction with Chestnut Mountain Trail, number 63. Wolf Ridge Trail goes left along Blue Ridge on the Tennessee Valley Divide and fifteen minutes later arrives at the site of the former Polk County Ramp Tramp, at 3,400 ft. elevation. This annual ramp cookout is now held each spring at Camp McCoy on Tenn. 30, 2 mi. north of U.S. 64.

The ramp is a member of the lily family, highly prized by mountain people as a "spring tonic." Another ramp festival is held at Cosby, Tennessee, once called the "Moonshine Capital of America."

From the Ramp Tramp site, the trail continues to the end on Big Frog Mountain and the start of the Big Frog Trail, number 64. Hiking time, sixteen minutes; elevation, 4,000 ft. The total distance from Pace Gap is 4.1 mi., according to a Forest Service engineer.

At left the Big Frog Trail follows a rocky ridge for twenty-nine minutes to the junction with Big Creek Trail, number 68. Turn left here down the Big Creek Trail to descend through a rhododendron "tunnel" fifteen minutes later. Beyond the thicket a few chestnut sprouts still fight the fungus disease that killed the forest giants in

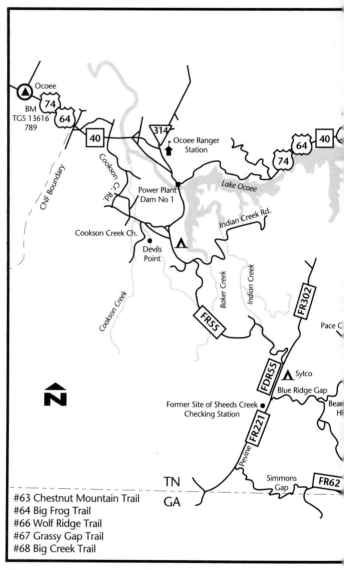

#63 Chestnut Mountain Trail
#64 Big Frog Trail
#66 Wolf Ridge Trail
#67 Grassy Gap Trail
#68 Big Creek Trail

Big Frog–Ocoee Ranger District

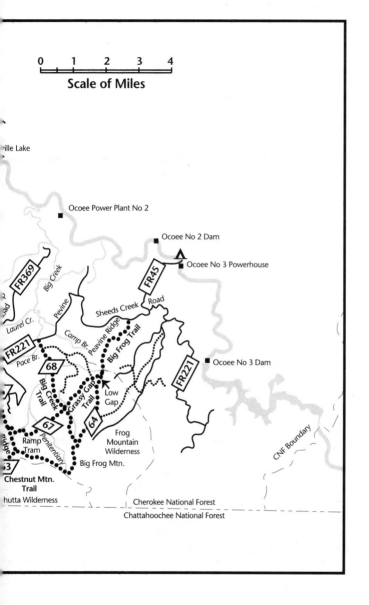

Scale of Miles

0 1 2 3 4

ille Lake

Ocoee Power Plant No 2

Ocoee No 2 Dam

Ocoee No 3 Powerhouse

FR369

Big Creek

FR45

Road

Sheeds Creek

Laurel Cr.

Pevine

Camp Br.

Peavine Ridge

Big Frog Trail

FR221

Pace Br.

68

Ocoee No 3 Dam

FR221

Big Creek Trail

Grassy Gap Trail

Low Gap

67

64

Ramp Tram

Penitentiary

Frog Mountain Wilderness

CNF Boundary

Big Frog Mtn.

3

Chestnut Mtn. Trail

hutta Wilderness

Cherokee National Forest

Chattahoochee National Forest

the 1920s. A view opens on the right as the trail switches to the left side of the ridge. Gentians bloom in the fall on this ridge. An hour and five minutes from the top of Big Frog Mountain, one might stop beside a branch for a snack. Leaving the branch, switch back northwest around the hill and arrive at a junction of trails beside a stream in a ravine twenty minutes later. A sign indicates the Grassy Gap Trail, and the path to the left leads 3 mi. to Grassy Gap.

The Big Creek Trail, number 68 straight ahead, crosses the toe of a ridge and drops downhill to a branch, then switches back northwest uphill and swings eastward across the ridge. The trail slopes down to another branch, then reverses up to the northwest to a beautiful valley view on the left. Half an hour from the last junction, the trail travels more directly north, ascending another hill for ten minutes to an unmarked trail junction. At the left fork it quickly crosses two branches with water in them and heads downhill at a rapid pace on an old roadbed. There is a short stretch where the trail takes a detour around a fallen tree, swings southwest (a view of the valley is on the left), and heads downhill again on an old road for fifteen minutes. At the entrance to the woods, there is a jeep road, FR 221J, which leads to FR 221, 2.4 mi. from the Big Frog sign. The total hiking time is five hours, twenty-five minutes. To get back to the starting point, turn left on FR 221 to 221E, another 2 mi., making the total trip 10.3 mi.

Chestnut Mountain Trail. Number 63. USGS Caney Creek quad, 126SE. Length 1.3 mi.; rating, moderate. The trailhead is located at the parking area for the Cohutta Wilderness, on the left of FR 62, Big Frog Road. Turn right off FR 221, 1.7 mi. east of Forest Development Road FDR 55, and travel 4.1 mi. to the parking area. The trail provides access to the wilderness and to the Wolf Ridge Trail, described above. It leaves the parking area at about 2,500 ft. elevation on a fairly easy grade on an old road, running northeast up the end of Chestnut Mountain to connect with the Wolf Ridge Trail at 3,100 ft. The trail follows an old road that was closed when the Cohutta Wilderness was established.

4. State Scenic Trails

The Tennessee Trails Systems Act, originally sponsored by the Tennessee Trails Association, was signed by Governor Winfield Dunn on April 28, 1971. The act called for the development of three classes of trails, which would be administered by the Department of Conservation. The trail system would include:

"(a) State Scenic Trails, which would be extended trails so located as to provide maximum potential for the appreciation of natural areas and for the conservation and enjoyment of the significant scenic, historic, natural, ecological, geological or cultural qualities of the areas through which such trails may pass." These trails were to be limited exclusively to foot use, except that horses and bicycles could be used on segments approved by the department.

"(b) State Recreation Trails, which will provide a variety of outdoor recreation uses in or reasonably accessible to urban areas." These could be foot, horse, or nonmotorized bicycle trails.

"(c) Connecting or side trails, which will provide additional points of public access to State Recreation or State Scenic Trails or which will provide connections between such trails. They shall be of the nature of the trails they serve."

The Tennessee Trails System Act designated seven state scenic trails, including the Appalachian Trail, the first of two national scenic trails designated by the National Trails System Act of 1968.

Appalachian Trail

The trail enters Tennessee near Damascus, Virginia, and follows the crest of the Appalachian Mountains along the Tennessee–North Carolina border; it cuts across a small section of North Carolina and again follows the state line southward through the Great

41

Smoky Mountains National Park, leaving Tennessee at Gregory Bald. Almost all of the AT outside the National Park lies on national forest land, a total of 108 mi. (173 km).

Trail of the Lonesome Pine

This is the next state scenic trail, taken from east to west. As spelled out in the Tennessee Trails System Act, it "begins near Corryton in Knox County thence running roughly the entire length, northeastward, of Grainger and Hawkins County, following closely the scenic gorges and escarpments of the Clinch Mountain range as the route is determined by the Department." The master plan for the trail was completed early in 1975, just before the Blanton administration in Nashville withdrew funds for the trail system. In 1977 the Department of Conservation managed to get limited funds and, with the help of the Tennessee Trails Association, resumed work on the section from Bean Gap to the Virginia state line. U.S. 25E passes through Bean Gap, which provided an alternate route to the Wilderness Road from the Holston Valley in pioneer days.

The Trail of the Lonesome Pine travelled along the crest of Clinch Mountain for a distance of 75 mi. The mountain crest, an average of 20 to 30 ft. wide, is characterized by large overhanging rock slabs and huge boulders. Views of the Great Smoky Mountains and the Cumberland Plateau offer the hiker a chance to appreciate the beauty of the Great Valley of Tennessee. The rock-strewn path, steep inclines up and down the gaps, and lack of water add up to make this trail one of the most difficult trails in the eastern United States. The trail started at the southern terminus of Clinch Mountain in Blaine, Tennessee, about 15 mi. northeast of Knoxville, and it was divided into six sections.

Politics killed the project. As we mentioned in chapter 2, opponents of condemnation proceedings caused the Department of Conservation to back off the project after sections 4 and 5 were officially opened. Development of sections 1 and 2 was blocked by a Knox County legislator who notified the commissioner that he would introduce a bill to abolish the Trail of the Lonesome Pine if work started on those sections. Maintenance of the trail was abandoned in 1984, and we don't recommend attempting to hike on this scenic trail, which has some of the best views in Tennessee.

Cumberland Trail

This is the next state scenic trail to the west and is the pilot project of the Tennessee Trails Association. It starts from Cumberland Gap, climbs to Tristate Peak, and mainly follows the eastern escarpment of the Cumberland Plateau to Prentice Cooper State Forest. Then it follows the rim of the "Grand Canyon of the Tennessee River" to the southern terminus in the town of Signal Mountain. The total hiking distance is more than 180 mi.

The Cumberland Trail route follows major fault lines created by the Allegheny orogeny 230 million years ago. It thus connects many dramatically scenic and historically important gaps including Cumberland, Emory, and Crab Orchard and the Tennessee River Gorge. Through these gaps from prehistoric times Native Americans crossed the highlands barrier on trading and raiding forays. Through them in the 1760s bold hunters from England's seaboard colonies first entered Kentucky and Tennessee, and by the early 1800s a growing stream of settlers was flowing into the Old Southwest.

The Cumberland Trail thus showcases geologic, scenic, and historical values of national significance. With this in mind Stan Murray, then Chairman of the Appalachian Trail Conference, suggested in 1969, at the Tennessee Trails Association's first annual meeting, the Cumberland Trail's inclusion in a spur off the A.T. down the Allegheny-Cumberland Front from Pennsylvania to Alabama. More recently, Russ Manning, in *The Historic Cumberland Plateau—An Explorer's Guide,* envisions the Cumberland Trail as part of a regional footpath that would allow you "to walk virtually the entire length of the Cumberland Plateau" from northern Kentucky to Gadsden, Alabama.

For administrative purposes, the Cumberland Trail is divided into nine sections. Because of State budget cutbacks by the McWherter administration, sections 1, 2, and 3, formerly managed by the Department of Environment and Conservation, have been unmaintained and, in effect, closed since 1990. Section 5, maintained infrequently by volunteers, is open but not well marked. (Section 5 maps are available at Cumberland Mountain State Park.) Sections 4, 6, 7, and 8 have never been completed.

Cumberland Trail: Section 9. Length, 13 mi.; rating, difficult. Location, Signal and Suck Creek mountains near the southern tip of the Cumberland range. Follow U.S. 127 to the town of Signal Mountain and follow the directional signs to Signal Point National Park parking area. The trail starts about halfway between the parking area and the Tennessee River Gorge Overlook. The trail follows bluff tops and ridges 1,800 and 2,000 ft. above sea level, drops into ravines lush with hemlocks towering over tangled growths of laurel and rhododendron, and crosses Middle, Julia, and Suck creeks. The view from Edwards Point covers a long stretch of the "Grand Canyon of the Tennessee," with historic Williams Island below on the left and the city of Chattanooga in the background.

The full length of Raccoon Mountain rises across the river from Edwards Point. The Tennessee River Canyon at this point was the scene of Chickamauga Indian attacks on the state's earliest white settlers traveling by flatboat to what is now Nashville. During the Civil War, soldiers signaled, via lookouts on the points or outcropping bluffs, from Signal Point to Edwards Point and so on down the canyon and around the bend to Bridgeport, Alabama.

Two primitive campsites are located on the first 11 mi. of the trail, and camping is permitted only at these sites. Parking areas at each end make it possible for backpackers to enjoy a one-way trip, stopping overnight at one of the campsites. It is difficult, if not impossible, to hike the 11 mi. in one day because the trail crosses several rock fields. Day hikes of interest are from Signal Point National Park to Middle Creek with a side trip to Rainbow Falls, a mighty rumbler in wet weather. This jaunt takes about three hours; six to eight hours are required to hike round trip from Signal Point to Edwards Point or from Signal Point one way via Edwards Point to Tenn. 27. Between Edwards Point and Tenn. 27, the trail follows the top of the bluffs some 2.5 mi. with beautiful views of the Suck Creek gorge, then drops down to a campsite on North Suck Creek. At this point the trail continues across a 225-ft. swinging bridge over North Suck Creek to Tenn. 27.

Starting on the Suck Creek Mountain side, look for the Prentice Cooper State Forest sign on Tenn. 27 and travel to the new parking lot near the fire tower. This section attracts many backpackers. It takes three to four hours to hike down to the roadside park on Suck Creek Road (Tenn. 27). Treats include vistas from high places, the Poplar Spring campsite (the water is potable), and abundant vegetation in interesting rock formations. Large jack-in-the-pulpits grow under the bluffs, and the purple rhododendron (*Rhododendron catawbiense*) blooms here a full month earlier than the same species on Roan Mountain.

An interesting side hike is available on a leg of the Cumberland Trail across Tenn. 27, starting at the roadside park (the present end of section 9). This leg consists of approximately 30 mi. of two loops in Prentice Cooper State Forest. Pot Point Loop Trail overlooks the Tennessee River canyon at many points, and Mullins Cove Loop includes spectacular views of Mullins Cove in the canyon. Maps of the Cumberland Trail and the loops are available from the Tennessee Department of Environment and Conservation, 7th Floor, L & C Tower, 401 Church St., Nashville, TN 37243-0446.

John Muir Trail

This is the fourth state scenic trail designated in the Tennessee Trails System Act. It runs northeastward from Pickett State Park headquarters parallel to Thompson Creek to a junction with the Sheltowee Trace near the Kentucky line. It turns south, then west across Divide Road, where there is parking. It follows No Business Creek several miles, angles to the southeast, and follows the Big South Fork River, crossing the Leatherwood Ford Bridge, to the old O&W Railroad Bridge. This section of the John Muir Trail is about 48 mi. in length. At 4.5 mi. SSE of the O&W Bridge, another section of the John Muir Trail, not yet connected to that just described, starts at Burnt Mill Bridge. It coincides with the counterclockwise leg of the Burnt Mill Bridge Loop Trail for 1.3 mi., where it branches off the Loop Trail to the right and proceeds about 2 mi. downstream paralleling Clear Fork. This section of the JMT is to be eventually extended to the O&W Bridge. A map of the Big South Fork is available at the Big South Fork National River and Recreation Area visitor's center. Right-of-way problems have blocked development between the Big South Fork and the Hiwassee State Scenic River. The south end of the John Muir Trail is described in chapter 3.

Trail of Tears

This trail, as designated in the Trails System Act, is not feasible as a hiking trail. The act was amended in the 1978 session of the General Assembly to make it a scenic route, with historic sites, scenic loops, and recreation trails pinpointed along the corridor.

In 1987 the Trail of Tears National Historic Trail was designated by Congress to be developed as an auto route connecting relevant historic sites. A National Park Service management and use plan for the T.O.T.N.H.T. shows four different historic land routes and a water route, the Tennessee River from Ross's Landing (Chattanooga) to the Ohio and the Mississippi. It indicates the northernmost land route as the most heavily traveled by the migrating Cherokee. With small divergences the T.O.T. State Scenic Trail follows this northern land route.

While funds are scarce, cooperative development of sites and signage by NPS and the State Department of Environment and Conservation for the Trail of Tears seems assured. Meanwhile, the City of Savannah in west Tennessee is planning a 700-ft. riverbank trail along the water route of the Trail of Tears as a demonstration project that can be emulated by other communities along the Tennessee River. Savannah's trail is designed for use by pedestrians, bicyclists, and the disabled and is to be built to NPS standards as an official interpretive component of the National Historic Trail.

The route of the State Scenic Trail starts from the Red Clay Council Grounds of the Cherokee at Red Clay State Historical Area in southern Bradley County. It follows TN-60 to Dayton; TN-30/284 to Fall Creek Falls State Park; TN-284, 111, and 8 to McMinnville; U.S.-70S to Murfreesboro; U.S.-231 to Lebanon; U.S.-70N to Hermitage; TN-45 to Whites Creek; U.S.-431 to Springfield; U.S.-41 to Adams; TN-76/238 to Port Royal; and TN-238 on to the Kentucky state line near Guthrie.

Hiking opportunities within the corridor include a 2.3-mi. loop trail at Red Clay, the Bowater trails near Dayton, Fall Creek Falls State Park, the Shellsford-Cardwell Mountain Trail near Cumberland Caverns, the Rutherford County Hike-Bike Complex, Cedars of Lebanon State Park, the Corps of Engineers trails around Percy Priest Reservoir, and a 1-mi. loop trail at Port Royal State Historical Area.

Shellsford-Cardwell Mountain Trail. Length, 8 mi.; rating, moderate. The Trail of Tears State Historical Route is a 260-mi. automobile tour that follows as closely as possible the route taken by the Cherokee Indians in the removal of 1838. This hiking trail is one of the several significant features along that route recognized by the Tennessee Department of Conservation for their interpretive value. The Shellsford Trail allows the hiker actually to walk in the steps of the Cherokees along an old stage road beside the beautiful Collins River.

The trail begins at the Cumberland Caverns parking area, 6 mi. east of McMinnville, a short distance off Tenn. 8. Interpretive literature and trail information can be obtained at the caverns office. In the first several hundred yards, the trail makes a gradual descent to the Collins River. Here the Cumberland Caverns Nature Trail, which has coincided with the Shellsford Trail to this point, turns back toward the caverns. The Shellsford Trail continues along the bank of the river for 2 mi. to the Shellsford Community. Here may be seen the ruins of the old gristmill where corn was ground for the Cherokees. A bridge across the river leads to the historic Shellsford Church, whose cemetery holds the remains of two Cherokee children, among the many who died of cold and disease on the 1838 trek.

From Shellsford the return to the parking area may be made over Cardwell Mountain, an outlier of the main Cumberland range. The 6-mi. return trail, with a vertical climb from the river of almost 1,000 ft., passes through hardwood forest. The top is notable for sandstone cliffs, and there is a panoramic view in winter when there is no foliage. Except for the area around Shellsford, the entire 8-mi. trail is devoid of pavement, power lines, and other forms of visual pollution.

Natchez Trace State Scenic Trail

The Trails System Act describes this trail as following closely the Natchez Trace Parkway from the Tennessee state line in Wayne County to Nashville, but development under the State Trails System Act has been given a low priority. The Natchez Trace National Scenic Trail, however, was authorized by Congress in 1983 as a hiking and horseback trail to be built within the Natchez Trace Parkway right-of-way. In 1988 the National Park Service initiated development in three separate prototype sections of about 20 mi. each in Tennessee, Alabama, and Mississippi. The Tennessee section of the Trail was completed in 1992 and is maintained primarily by volunteers under the leadership of the Natchez Trace Trail Conference, Inc. It is described in chapter 7.

The Natchez Trace Parkway, a unit of the National Park Service, was created in 1938 as a motor route to closely follow the course of the original trace. To date over 90 percent of the parkway's 102 miles in Tennessee has been built and opened to the public.

Chickasaw Bluffs Trail

This trail, the seventh designated in the Trails System Act, is to run roughly from T. O. Fuller State Park south of Memphis to Fort Pillow State Park in Lauderdale County and, continuing northward, will terminate at Reelfoot Lake State Park. Implementation of this trail was halted in 1975 because of problems with the landowners, but short sections were laid out in Meeman-Shelby Forest Day Use Park and Fort Pillow State Park. The first Chickasaw Bluff, site of Fort Prud'homme, built by the French explorer La Salle in 1682, is at Fort Pillow. Memphis is located on the fourth Chickasaw Bluff.

Overmountain Victory Trail

This is an eighth state scenic trail, which was added to the system by the 90th General Assembly. It is a segment of the Overmountain Victory National Historic Trail created by Congress in 1980. It follows the route of the volunteer army that marched from the Sycamore Shoals on the Watauga River to help defeat the British in the Battle of Kings Mountain. The trail almost totally follows roads and highways that now lie along this 200-mile route from Abingdon, Virginia, to Kings Mountain National Military Park in South Carolina. In Tennessee, however, 2 miles of the route is a hiking trail. It extends from the end of Sugar Hollow Road in Roan Mountain State Park up a steep grade (1,300 ft. elevation change) to a juncture with the Appalachian Trail at Yellow Mountain Gap. Annually, during the last week of September and the first week of October, the Overmountain Victory Trail Association, Inc. sponsors a family-oriented reenactment and march along this entire historic trail route. For information on the 2-mi. hiking trail, write Roan Mountain State Park, Rte. 1, Box 236, Roan Mountain, TN 37687, or call (615) 772–3303. For information on the annual reenactment, write Sycamore Shoals State Park, Elizabethton, TN 37643, or call (615) 543–5808.

5. Trails in State Parks

In 1977 there were 117 trails in Tennessee state parks, and trail development was going forward at a rapid pace. From 1977 to 1987 at least ten new parks were added to the system. Among the newer parks, Roan Mountain, famous for purple rhododendron (*Rhododendron catawbiense*), has an excellent system, including ski trails, connecting with the Appalachian Trail and adjacent national forests in Tennessee and North Carolina. Today state parks contain two hundred trails totaling about 650 mi. in length. We describe some of the best of these trails in areas with the greatest public interest, because of special geographic location, scenic values, or vacation opportunities.

Big Ridge State Park

Located on Norris Lake, the park is accessible via Tenn. 61, either northeast from I-75 at the Clinton-Norris interchange or west from Tenn. 33 north of Knoxville. The latter approach is not recommended for travel-trailer traffic. Some of the best state park trails in Tennessee are in Big Ridge. There is a great diversity of plant life and wildlife, including deer, ruffed grouse, chipmunks, squirrels, raccoons, and a variety of bird life. Windstorms in the late seventies toppled many beetle-killed pines and some hardwood trees. They have been cleared from the trails by state park crews.

Big Valley Trail. Length, 6 mi.; rating, moderate. The trail starts from a park road 100 yds. east of the superintendent's residence and the parking area for the Old Mill, elevation 1,050 ft. It starts in open pine woods, climbs a gentle rise, and descends through a thicket to cross a shaded glen. Next it ascends a long slope with a deep ravine on the right. In 1987 trail crews restored

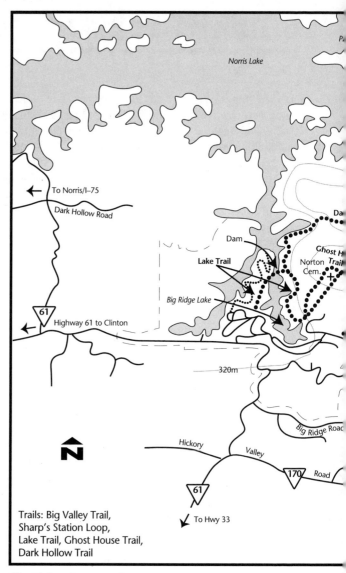

Norris Lake

To Norris/I–75

Dark Hollow Road

Dam

Lake Trail

Da

**Ghost H
Norton Trail
Cem.**

Big Ridge Lake

61 Highway 61 to Clinton

320m

N

Big Ridge Road

Hickory Valley Road

61 170

To Hwy 33

Trails: Big Valley Trail,
Sharp's Station Loop,
Lake Trail, Ghost House Trail,
Dark Hollow Trail

Big Ridge State Park

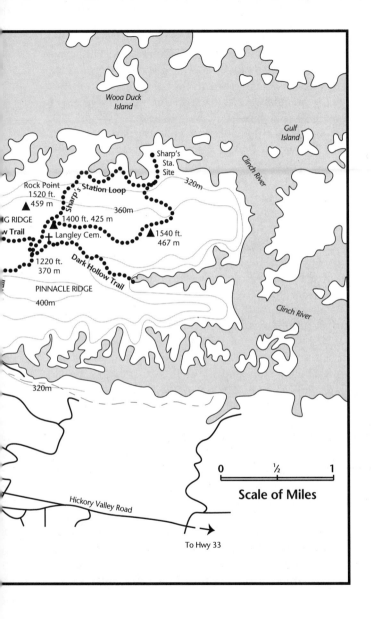

Wooa Duck
Island

Gulf
Island

Clinch River

Sharp's
Sta.
Site

320m

Rock Point
1520 ft.
▲ 459 m

Sharp's Station Loop

G RIDGE

360m

w Trail

1400 ft. 425 m

✝ Langley Cem.

▲ 1540 ft.
467 m

1220 ft.
370 m

Dark Hollow Trail

PINNACLE RIDGE

400m

Clinch River

320m

0   ½   1

Scale of Miles

Hickory Valley Road

To Hwy 33

the tread where tree roots had been exposed and where it was eroded. The trail crosses a low saddle and descends into a little valley through lush ferns, then crosses another glen with a footbridge over a tiny stream. Poison ivy grows in the valley, and pink lady's slippers bloom in abundance. (This description was taken in May.) The trail climbs a sharp rise for a few yards, followed by a long, easy slope on a broad hillside through open woods; the pines are giving way to young hardwoods—dogwood, tulip poplar, maple, elm, and other species. The Ghost House Trail intersects the path about 0.5 mi. from the trailhead. The trail becomes steeper for 100 yds. and moves into a mixed pine-hardwood forest as it ascends the toe of Pinnacle Ridge. At the top, near 1,400 ft. elevation, the trail follows the side of the ridge overlooking a deep valley on the right.

There is a gradual descent to a narrow saddle, and the trail switches to the left side of the ridge. After about 200 yds. it passes a windfall and drops sharply. The trail swings to the right around the end of the ridge and passes another blowdown. Yellow star grass blooms along the trail, which passes through a patch of crested dwarf iris before crossing a low dome to the saddle at the Dark Hollow Trail intersection at 1,220 ft. There is a steep ascent to Big Ridge, where trees toppled by storms lie on top of the sharp ridge. There is a slight drop, and the trail cuts through a bigger windfall before a longer climb. The trail passes to the left of the old Langley Cemetery, where the only modern gravestone marks the resting place of young Edward Loy, who died in 1932 at the age of six. All the other graves are marked with fieldstones at the head and foot—no inscriptions. The trail becomes steeper, levels out briefly, then steepens again before leveling out on top of Big Ridge at about 1,400 ft. elevation.

A trail to the left in open woods goes to Rock Point, the second highest spot in the park, at 1,520 ft. A short distance beyond here is the junction with Sharp's Station Loop, which runs down a spur of the ridge to the north. The trail swings to the right past a big hollow oak tree and climbs a point on a rock-strewn path. Red blazes mark the path as it follows the crest of Big Ridge to the northeast, rising gradually to 1,460 ft. A clump of squawroot has pushed through the forest litter on the left. After the trail drops through another saddle and climbs back to 1,470 ft., Norris Lake is visible through a break in the trees on the left as the trail follows a hogback ridge to Indian Rock. A plaque marks the spot where Indians ambushed and scalped pioneer Peter Graves in 1794.

The highest point in the park, 1,540 ft., is farther along the ridge to the northeast. The Big Valley Trail ends a short distance past Indian Rock, and the east end of the **Sharp's Station Loop** plunges down a steep slope to the left, with no switchbacks. This section was scheduled for upgrading in 1988. It levels out on a spur with three big white oak trees at the far edge, drops on down through a cedar glade, and swings right to a junction where a sign announces the "Trail to Rock Point." The right fork crosses a little stream on a rock ledge, jogs right about 10 ft., and follows another ledge about 50 yds. After curving left, the trail parallels the shoreline of a cove at the left to a plaque marking the site of Sharp's Station, one of the first two settlements west of the Appalachians. The other was the James White Fort, which became Knoxville. All that remains of Sharp's Station are a few stone fences. Returning to the forks of the trail, the loop continues westward along the lakeshore. It turns southward through the cedars, rising to the hardwood forest, and climbs the ridge back to the junction with the Big Valley Trail. The length of the loop is between 2 and 3 mi.

Lake Trail, **Dark Hollow**, **Big Valley Loop.** Total estimated length, about 5 mi.; rating, moderate; elevation change, about 350 ft. This loop starts at the group camp on the Lake Trail, the oldest trail in the park, dating back to the 1930s. Leaving the group camp at about 1,080 ft. elevation, the trail crosses a little stream on a footbridge, passes through a thicket, and crosses a small spring branch that flows through a tile. The trail turns left about 100 yds. from the trailhead, and the Ghost House Trail goes straight ahead. The Lake Trail crosses a marsh, a short rise, and then another marsh about 50 yds. wide. The trail leads uphill through cedars and pines, with hardwood undergrowth coming up among the dead and dying pines, then crosses a low ridge through mixed hardwoods. Blueberries grow along the next section of the trail, which now follows the shore of Big Ridge Lake.

Leaving the lake, the trail follows a gentle rise parallel to a small stream for about 200 yds., crosses a shallow draw, then the toe of a low ridge, and curves back to the left along the ridge. It crosses another shallow valley with a smaller stream, rises 50 ft. through windfall, then turns back to the right through deeper woods to twin coves, almost 90 degrees to each other, draining into the lake. In deep woods there are tulip, maple, and some pine. The trail rounds the end of a cove and comes back to the lakeshore. A rutted section here was upgraded in 1987. Around the hill is Big Ridge Dam, with Norris Lake lapping at its foot. The dam was built in CCC days to form Big Ridge Lake. The Lake Trail crosses the dam.

The Dark Hollow Trail, marked with blue blazes, starts from the west end of the dam on a narrow path. Following the shoreline of Norris Lake, the trail rises sharply past mountain laurel, passes a windfall, and winds around a steep hillside. The trail turns right up a hollow, leads over a low hill for 0.3 mi., then crosses the head of a deep ravine and the toe of Pinnacle Ridge. In deep woods less wind damage appears. There is a steep descent into another ravine and a shorter climb over the next ridge before the trail crosses a stream running into a small cove in Norris Lake and arrives at the old Dark Hollow Road. The road has been closed since the impoundment of Norris Lake in 1937.

The old Dark Hollow Road parallels the stream, with open woods on both sides. Passing a couple of spring branches, the trail begins a gradual rise, getting farther away from the stream, and is surrounded by tall second-growth hardwoods—dogwood, white oak, maple, tulip, hickory—and much poison ivy. It crosses a marshy area and turns sharply to the right around the head of the stream. The old road winds around the end of a ridge and crosses the Big Valley Trail in the saddle between Pinnacle and Big ridges. The Dark Hollow Trail follows the old road down another stream to Dark Hollow Cove on Norris Lake, a distance of about 1 mi.

Continuing around the loop, the Big Valley Trail heads right across Pinnacle Ridge, drops down to the Ghost House Trail, a distance of about a mile, and turns right. The trail slopes upward about 200 yds., then downward along a shoulder below the ridgetop, passing through a dogwood thicket and a massive windfall. Farther down the ridge, the old Norton Cemetery lies on the right. The gravestones are thin marble slabs of the early twentieth century. The trail slopes downward gently along an old roadbed on top of a narrow ridge, crosses a low saddle, and continues down the toe of the ridge among dying pines, with the hardwood undergrowth developing rapidly. The Ghost House Trail ends at the Lake Trail, and the starting point at the group camp is 100 yds. to the left.

Frozen Head State Park and Natural Area

The park is located in the eastern part of Morgan County. The access road turns north off Tenn. 62, 2 mi. east of the junction of U.S. 27 and Tenn. 62 at Wartburg. This park, the former Morgan State Forest, is managed jointly as a state park and natural area. It has one of the finest trail systems in Tennessee. Developments include the trail system, picnic areas with rest rooms and running water, a primitive campground limited to tents and folding trailers, an outdoor amphitheater, visitor's center, and personnel housing. Frozen Head State Natural Area includes several of the highest peaks in the Cumberland Mountains, with their connecting ridges and interlaced valleys. They are the eroded remnants of the Cumberland Plateau, but, because the stratigraphic basin lying immediately beneath them retarded their erosion relative to the rest of the Plateau, they remain much higher than the adjacent area to the south and west. The mountains, of sedimentary origin, are composed of alternate layers of sandstone and shale, with intervening layers of coal.

The massive layers of sandstone provide many of the more at-

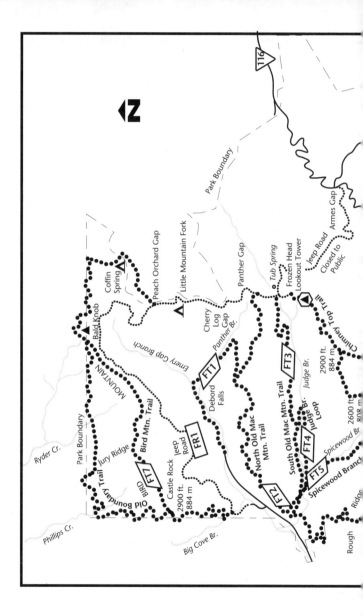

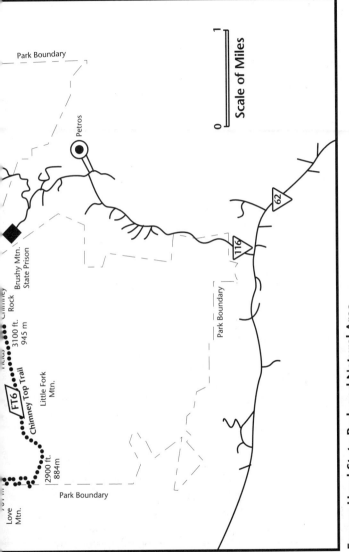

Park Boundary

Petros

Brushy Mtn.
State Prison

Chimney
Rock

3100 ft.
945 m

FT6

Chimney Top Trail

Little Fork
Mtn.

2900 ft.
884 m

Love
Mtn.

Park Boundary

Park Boundary

116

62

0   1

Scale of Miles

Frozen Head State Park and Natural Area

tractive features of the park, such as the great cap rocks, the rock houses, and the massive boulders in the narrow valleys. Rock enthusiasts will find small waterfalls, rock houses in the undercut bluff, or fine overlooks at the top of the bluffline, which can be followed for miles with relative ease.

Topo USGS quad sheets covering the park include Camp Austin, 122 SE; Gobey, 122NE; Fork Mountain, 129NW; and Petros, 129SW. Trail maps are available at park headquarters or from the Tennessee Department of Environment and Conservation, 7th Floor, L&C Tower, 401 Church Street, Nashville, TN 37243-0446. The trails are color-coded, and the color of the marker, length, and name of each trail are noted in the legend on the map. Many more interesting features may be found off the trails by those experienced in using topo maps. A permit is required for cross-country hiking or hiking on closed trails. All the developed trails are in the northern end of the park. They have been arranged to form loops and were all refurbished and upgraded between 1985 and 1988. Many miles of trails in the southern portion of the park have not been maintained in recent years. Only experienced hikers with good map-reading skills should try these overgrown trails. This is copperhead and rattlesnake country, but there is little danger of being bitten if ordinary precautions are used. Be careful around rocks, fallen trees, and old logs.

There is a shortage of water during late summer and fall. Springs are not plentiful, nor as large as those in the Smokies. All trails in Frozen Head are rocky, and some are fairly rough, requiring sturdy shoes for hiking. A turned ankle or a bruised foot can ruin a hike very quickly. Most of the trails start from a common trailhead parking lot near the picnic area on Flat Fork Creek.

Panther Branch Trail. Color code, blue dot; length, 2 mi.; rating, moderate. This trail starts at the gate, at the old concrete bridge across the north prong of Flat Fork Creek, slightly more than 0.5 mi. upstream from the picnic area, elevation 1,400 ft. A parking area is provided at the end of the road. The first mile follows an old road along the creek, with many boulders along the road and in the creek. Many people enjoy wading in the stream in spring and summer. One-half mile from the beginning, an overlook has been built at DeBord Falls, with steps leading to the bottom of the falls. In winter many large clumps of evergreen sedges and Christmas ferns can be seen on the north slope across the stream. Just upstream from the junction of Panther Branch and the creek, at 1,800 ft. elevation, the trail drops down a high bank and crosses the north prong of Flat Fork, entering a flat area of about one acre. This was the location of a logging camp more than a half century ago. The left trail follows a switchback railroad bed up Emory Gap Branch to a waterfall. Panther Branch Trail swings back right, soon picks up an old railroad bed, and follows it a few hundred yards to the crossing of Panther Branch.

Hundreds of people visit this area every weekend in April to view one of the finest spring wildflower shows in the country. The trail begins to climb rather steeply at this point and soon is a considerable distance above the stream. It crosses a very thick outcropping of black shale exposed in a cascade in a small stream. The footing is narrow here for a short distance, becoming steep and rocky. Panther Branch is a series of small waterfalls in the upper reaches of its watershed. About 0.3 mi. above the cascade, the trail turns sharply, leaves the stream at 2,200 ft., and passes through a hardwood forest that faces directly north. An abundance of wildflowers bloom on this mountain slope in spring. Approximately 0.5 mi. after leaving Panther Branch, the trail ends at the North Old Mac Mountain Trail at 2,500 ft. To the right, this trail leads back to the trailhead. A high rock overlook is located about 200 yds. to the north of the junction.

North Old Mac Mountain Trail. Color code, red dot; length, 3.6 mi.; rating, moderate. This trail starts from the main trailhead parking lot, passing through a nice pine plantation on nearly level ground. About 0.3 mi. after leaving the trailhead, the trail makes a 90-degree turn to the left. The Spicewood Branch Trail continues straight ahead. A few yards farther the trail turns to the left again and starts to climb around the western end of Old Mac Mountain at 1,500 ft. elevation. After rounding the end, the trail follows the north side of the mountain to the northeast, alternately going around small ridges and dropping into large north coves. The trees and other plants on this north slope provide shade, making this an ideal summer trail. During the hotter months this trail is much more comfortable than those on the south side of the mountain.

About 2.2 mi. after leaving the trailhead, this trail reaches the junction with the Panther Branch Trail at 2,500 ft. elevation. Just prior to the junction, there is a designated backpack campsite. A short trail to the left leads to a high rock overlook on the point of a ridge. From the junction the Old Mac Mountain Trail leads almost due east, and the ridges and coves of the lower reaches are almost absent. The constant north slope makes an ideal habitat for wildflowers, and many fine displays can be found in April all along the trail in these upper reaches. On the north slopes of Old Mac Mountain and in Panther Branch Valley at the foot of the slope, a superior strain of tulip (yellow) poplar has evolved. Several of these trees have been selected by the Department of Forestry at the University of Tennessee as a source of genetic material to be used in establishing seed orchards.

Near the junction with the jeep road, a spur trail leads to Panther Gap Rock House. Three-fourths of a mile above the intersection with the Panther Branch Trail, a prominent line of sandstone bluffs will be seen above the trail. Some interesting fossils can be seen on the underside of the overhanging rock. It is illegal to remove such articles from the site. Spring wildflowers are abundant around the base of this line of bluffs. A few minutes' hike from the bluffs reaches into Panther Gap. Tub Spring is about 0.3 mi. to the right, and the Frozen Head lookout tower is about 0.3 mi. beyond the intersection of the road near the spring.

Along the approach to the intersection, the road to the left, leading down to Tenn. 116 at Armes Gap, has been closed to the public. The tower on top of Frozen Head Mountain is the highest point in the park, 3,324 ft. elevation. It provides spectacular views of the high country to the east and the Tennessee River Valley to the southwest. On a clear day the Tennessee Valley, Great Smoky Mountains, and Cumberland Plateau are visible in the distance.

South Old Mac Mountain Trail. Color code, yellow dot; length, 2.8 mi.; rating, moderate. From the trailhead parking lot, this trail coincides with the North Old Mac Mountain Trail. About 200 yds. beyond the North Old Mac trailhead, just before the bridge across Judge Branch, the trail angles to the left and enters an attractive hemlock grove. Three-fourths of a mile farther up the trail, it connects with the Judge Branch Loop, an extension of the former Wildflower Trail, 1.7 mi. from the Spicewood Branch Trail. From the hemlock grove, it stays in the valley a few hundred yards before beginning to climb the south slope of the mountain. One point of interest along this first section is an old building with thick walls. It was used to store explosives during the construction of trails in the 1930s. From the old explosives storehouse to the top of the mountain, the trail has a southern exposure. It is an excellent winter trail when the warm rays of sun are welcome, but this exposure makes it a hot summer trail. However, the southern exposure makes this one of the best trails when looking for early spring wildflowers. Several of the earlier species begin blooming by mid-March.

This trail is the shortest route between park headquarters and the tower on top of the mountain. Many hikers use one of the longer trails to reach the top and descend by the more direct route. The trail comes out at the road intersection near Tub Spring at 3,000 ft. To the right the road leads to the Frozen Head lookout tower.

Spicewood Branch Trail. Color code, purple dot; length, 2.5 mi.; rating, difficult. This trail also leaves the parking lot on the same route as the Old Mac Mountain trails. One-tenth of a mile beyond the turnoff from the South Old Mac Mountain Trail, the Judge Branch Loop leads to the left. The former Wildflower Trail has been extended across a bridge on Judge Branch and circles to the left to a junction with the South Old Mac Mountain Trail. This is one of the easiest trails in the park, and its attractions include the great white trillium, huge beech trees, a hemlock grove, and moss-covered fieldstone bridge abutments. Continuing straight ahead from the junction, the Spicewood Branch Trail follows an old road about 0.3 mi., passing some large hemlock trees growing along Spicewood Branch. Just above the last of the hemlocks, the trail leaves the old roadbed near a small branch crossing at 1,700 ft. elevation, then turns at a right angle, proceeding directly up the mountainside. There is a campsite at the foot of the mountain. This section was not a part of the original trail but was put to use as a shortcut between the graded trail and the old road it follows on the lower end. Fortunately, this section is short, and the trail soon gets back on the graded tread. It passes through several north-facing coves as it works its way up the mountain, crossing the headwaters of Spicewood Branch (now little more than a deep cove).

The trail rounds a west-facing point at 2,650 ft. elevation, leaving the Spicewood Branch drainage. A short distance beyond this point, the trail crosses some of the steepest slopes in the park. Three-fourths of a mile from the point, the trail ends at the Chimney Top Trail, on top of the ridge at 2,900 ft. Frozen Head tower is 1 mi. to the left, and Mart Fields Spring and campsite are 0.8 mi. to the right. The Spicewood Branch Trail is a good summer trail, mostly on north slopes which make cooler hiking. The woods are more attractive than those found along some of the other trails.

Chimney Top Trail. Color code, green dot; length, 6.9 mi.; rating, difficult. The trail leaves the main trailhead and visitor's center parking lot at 1,400 ft., skirts park headquarters, and ascends the north slope of Rough Ridge along the park boundary. It crosses the rocky crest at 2,300 ft., about 1.8 mi. from the trailhead. It now descends into the upper end of Rocky Fork Creek, 1,950 ft. elevation. Near the bottom of this valley, the trail crosses an old logging railroad grade. Exploration of this grade will show the ingenious methods used by the early loggers to get their trains into the mountains, by use of switchbacks in the roadbeds.

From Rocky Fork the trail leads up the north slope of Love Mountain, passing through some nice woods in a deep cove. Near the top of Love Mountain there is a spring just uphill to the right of the trail, marked by a small hemlock growing in moist soil. The water may or may not be potable, depending on how well the spring has been cleaned out. The trail leaves the old constructed trail bed at the top of the ridge at 2,900 ft. and makes a sharp left turn off the ridge, which is fairly level here. A few hundred yards after leaving the graded trail bed, the trail climbs directly up the point of the ridge. The last half-mile is a strenuous climb to Chimney Rock, 3,100 ft. elevation. This segment of the trail is listed as only 3.4 mi. in length, but by the time you reach the top of Chimney Rock, it seems twice that far. There is a campsite here, but no water.

Inexperienced climbers have only one way to the top of this great boulder. Approach the rock, turn left, and follow its base to the northeast corner, watching for a trail that can be used to get to the top by pulling oneself up on trees and shrubs growing out of cracks in the rocks. Be cautious when climbing, as rattlesnakes have been seen around the rocks during the summer months. On a clear, crisp day the view from the top is ample reward for the strenuous effort it takes to get there. To the north are the Cumberlands; to the northwest the Cumberland Plateau extends as far as the eye can see. To the west the Crab Orchard Mountains stand out in bold relief; to the southeast the Tennessee Valley with its TVA lakes is visible; and to the east are the Smokies! Mount Le Conte and Clingman's Dome are easily recognizable.

Chimney Rock is the largest of several ancient cap rocks to be found along the crest of Chimney Top Mountain. Exploring some of these remains, particularly in seasons when snakes are not active, can provide an enjoyable experience. From Chimney Rock, the trail passes near several cap rock formations, descending to a narrow gap at 2,750 ft. It passes through the gap and ascends along a broken line of sandstone bluffs to the ridgetop. The terrain flattens in a young forest at the site of an old mountain farm known as Mart Fields. The trail follows the ridge to a campsite with a spring that provides water year-round. From Mart Fields the trail continues along the original CCC trail, following the foot of the bluff along the east side of Mart Knob to the junction with the Spicewood Branch Trail.

From the junction, the trail follows the road along the crest of the mountain at about 3,000 ft. and swings left around the west side of Frozen Head Peak to the intersection with the road to the lookout tower, which is maintained and provides an excellent platform for photographers. Here is some of the most spectacular scenery in Tennessee. To the left the road leads to Tub Spring and a campsite with a stone fireplace built by CETA labor in 1978. An Adirondack shelter is planned here. Beyond Tub Spring, the old road down to Armes Gap on Tenn. 116 has been gated and is closed to the public.

Bird Mountain Trail. Color code, white dot; length, 4 mi.; rating, difficult. This trail is closed for maintenance on the section that lies on the north slope of Bird Mountain. The Bird Mountain Trail, formerly part of the Boundary Trail, is a circuitous route that offers an opportunity for a two-day or three-day backpacking experience. It connects with the Chimney Top Trail at Tub Spring to form a 15-mi. loop. The average hiker should allow two days to complete the circuit, since the first few miles is a series of steep climbs and sharp descents. From the trailhead parking lot at 1,400 ft. to Squire Knob at 3,100 ft., a hiker will climb a total of 4,400 ft. and descend a total of 1,700 ft. in a distance of about 6 mi. There are elevation changes up to 1,200 ft. in relatively short distances.

Leaving the trailhead parking area, cross the bridge to the north and follow the old jeep road for several hundred yards past the campground to the first small stream crossing. The trail leaves the old road and works its way up the side of Bird Mountain through a total of fourteen switchbacks. This trail crosses the park boundary line onto private property part of the time. It arrives at the top of the mountain (2,900 ft. elevation) about 2 mi. from the trailhead. Just to the right at the crest is Castle Rock, the most massive cap rock in the park, nearly 0.5 mi. long. It contains several interesting rock houses and small sandstone "caves." There is an overlook on top of the bluff with an outstanding view of Panther Branch Watershed and Frozen Head Mountain.

From here the trail was rerouted in 1992 to follow the crest of Bird Mountain to Bald Knob. There are spectacular views from the ridgetops along this route, and the trail is less rugged than the original route, on which maintenance has been discontinued. A few hardy hikers, preferring the greater challenge, may continue to use the old trail. A permit is required to use closed trails. Elevations range from 2,800 to 3,000 ft., and the ups and downs are less strenuous. The trail passes around the north side of Bald Knob at about 3,100 ft.

The old Boundary Trail drops off the top of Bird Mountain into a large north cove, the upper end of Phillips Creek Watershed, which is an outstanding area for spring wildflowers. The woods are very beautiful here, but much of them are on private land, and the timber may be cut at any time. The trail continues down Phillips Creek to the corner of the park at about 1,400 ft. elevation, turns east, and almost immediately starts to climb Jury Ridge. After a rugged climb to the top of Jury Ridge (2,300 ft. elevation), the trail continues around the north slope of the mountain and crosses the upper watershed of Rayder Creek. From Rayder Creek it begins the long climb up Bald Knob.

Back on the Bird Mountain Trail, from Bald Knob it descends into a north cove, passes around the point of a ridge, and then descends into the extreme upper reaches of the Emory River Valley. A short distance from the valley, the trail turns onto an old overgrown road that it follows up the mountain to Coffin Spring and another campsite, at 2,900 ft. From there it follows the route of the jeep road through Peach Orchard Gap to a campsite on Little Fork Mountain, then through Cherry Log Gap and Panther Gap to Tub Spring. From there the return to the trailhead follows the Chimney Top Trail, or if the hiker has had enough by now, he or she can take the shorter route via the South Old Mac Mountain Trail. It's downhill most of the way.

Pickett State Park and Pickett State Forest

Both park and forest are located on Tenn. 154 about 10 mi. northeast of Jamestown off U.S. 127. From U.S. 27, to the east, follow Tenn. 297 (Leatherwood Ford Road) from Oneida across the Big South Fork National River and Recreation Area to Tenn. 154 and turn right.

There are 33 mi. of day-use trails in Pickett State Park. Camping is restricted to park campgrounds. In addition, the Sheltowee Trace National Recreation Trail, formerly the Great Meadow Trail, and the John Muir State Scenic Trail have been extended to park headquarters. There are fourteen trails to choose from, all interconnected, making it possible to begin at one end and hike all the trails in series. There is a great diversity along the way in both vegetation and landscape. Several places on the trails offer a true feeling of wilderness. Most trails are connected to the main park area at some point, and many of them have rest shelters along the way. These shelters were originally built by the CCC in the early 1930s and are mainly constructed of logs from the American chestnut (*Castanea dentata*).

There is a vast territory of wild land surrounding Pickett State Park and Forest. Hundreds of miles of jeep roads and foot trails traverse the area. The Sheltowee Trace National Recreation Trail connects Pickett's trails with those of the Daniel Boone National Forest in Kentucky. Pickett adjoins the Big South Fork Area, developed by the U.S. Army Corps of Engineers and managed by the National Park Service. There are more than 200 mi. of hiking trails in the Big South Fork. U.S.G.S. topographic quadrangle maps that cover this area are Bell Farm, KY; Barthell SW, TN; Sharp Place, TN; and Pall Mall, TN. These are recommended for planning trips into this area and may be obtained by writing to the Tennessee Division of Geology, L&C Tower 401 Church Street, Nashville, TN 37243, and to the Kentucky Geological Survey, Lexington, KY 40506, for the Kentucky map.

Only two trails from Pickett State Park are described in this guide. All other trails, except the Sheltowee Trace National Recreation Trail, are color-coded for easier identification as listed below.

Natural Bridge Trail, brown 1.5-mi. loop, easy walking; Indian Rockhouse Trail, orange, 0.5 mi. one way, easy; Hazard Cave Trail, white, 2.5-mi. loop, medium difficulty; Ridge Trail, green, 3-mi. loop, medium difficulty; Lake View Trail, gray, 0.8-mi. loop, easy walking; Bluff Trail, yellow, 1 mi. one way, easy; Ladder Trail, brown, 1-mi. loop, medium to difficult; Island Trail, blue, 1-mi. loop, easy; Double Falls Trail, white, 1 mi. one way, medium to difficult; Tunnel Trail, no blazes, 1 mi. one way, medium to difficult; Coffee Trail, orange, 2 mi. one way, medium to difficult.

Hidden Passage Trail. Color code, green; length, 8 mi.; rating easy. A trail for all seasons, this loop follows the 1,500-ft. contour above Thompson Creek. Thompson Creek is a clear stream of spring water that oozes continually from a 300-ft.-thick sandstone filter, the Cumberland Plateau. Sometimes the sounds of a mighty rushing torrent may be heard from the trail, but at other times a hiker must peer over the edge of the bluff to be sure there is still water in the stream. The trail reverses on the ridge above the confluence of Thompson and Rock creeks. Rock Creek is another clear mountain stream rushing northward into Kentucky to the Cumberland River. For several miles the trail winds along the 1,600-ft. contour above Rock Creek and then returns across a flat ridge to its origin. The Hidden Passage Trail is so named because of a natural sandstone tunnel through a bluff.

There are two spur trails off the main trail. One is the Double Waterfalls, an exciting, one-way, 1-mi. walk from a dry forest setting to the rhododendron- and viburnum-covered banks of Thompson Creek. During early spring this trail boasts many wildflowers, with such species as pinxter flower, mayapple, bloodroot, *Trillium flexipes,* and at least five species of violets, to name a few. The other spur is the Tunnel Trail, a winding 1-mi. path through the shade of eastern hemlock, big-leafed magnolia, and tulip poplar to an old railroad tunnel on Rock Creek. The tunnel is unsafe for entry, but it is interesting to stand outside and imagine the

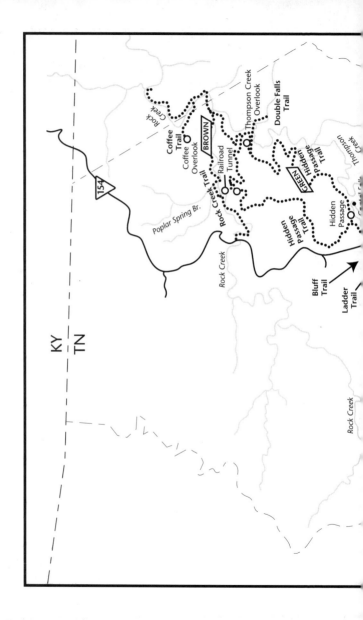

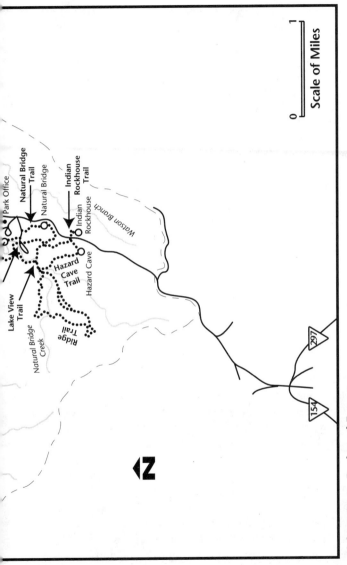

Pickett State Park and Forest

Scale of Miles

0   1

N

Park Office

Natural Bridge Trail

Natural Bridge

Indian Rockhouse Trail

Indian Rockhouse

Watson Branch

Lake View Trail

Hazard Cave Trail

Hazard Cave

Natural Bridge Creek

Ridge Trail

297

154

labors of the rugged men who built this tunnel in the last century.

The Hidden Passage Trail is a trail for all seasons because of its rugged beauty and interesting variety of botanical species visible all through the year. During the winter while the deciduous forest is clothed in somber brown, there is still a goodly number of evergreens to keep the freshness of spring. Then, as winter storms begin, the white cover of snow gives the landscape a cheerful, welcoming appeal. On the ridges, generally above 1,500 ft. elevation, there are shortleaf and Virginia pine. Down in the valleys are the eastern hemlock and white pine. There are many other evergreen plants that add to the winter beauty along the trail. The ground is covered with trailing arbutus, boxwood, huckleberry, and partridgeberry. Interlacing clumps of teaberry, two species of lycopodium, and a fair sprinkling of lichens and mosses add to the allure. Between the trees and ground cover, there is much mountain laurel, rhododendron, and American holly.

There are wild hog tracks and signs of deer scrounging for acorns beneath the snow. In the early morning hours, it is common to see one of the many barred owls that live in Pickett Forest. The pileated woodpecker and the red-cockaded woodpecker have been seen there.

Like clockwork each March, as the vernal equinox arrives so do the white blossoms of the trailing arbutus and the pale blue of the bluets, which are followed in continuous succession by an array of wildflowers throughout the summer and into the fall. Some of the rarest of these gems are the grass of parnassus and the round-leaved catchfly, both of which can be seen near the trail. These are only a few of the highlights of the Hidden Passage Trail.

Rock Creek Trail. Color code, brown; length, about 5 mi.; rating, medium. This one-way trail runs from Thompson Creek Overlook on the Hidden Passage Trail to Tenn. 154, 3.5 mi. north of park headquarters, Sharp Place USGS quad, 335 SE. Actually, the Rock Creek Trail starts about 0.3 mi. from the overlook, but that point makes a natural starting place for this hike. Down the side of a ridge the trail crosses a branch on a slippery log and follows a switchback path up to the junction. The Rock Creek Trail goes to the right, a fairly level path on a broad ridge for 0.3–0.5 mi., drops down the toe of the ridge 200 yds., follows a shelf along a bluff another 200 yds., and then slopes down to Thompson Creek and the confluence with Rock Creek.

Turning left up Rock Creek, the trail crosses to the junction with the Coffee Trail in the shade of yellow and sweet birches and cucumber magnolia trees. The trail goes left from the junction, follows a rocky bluff, and crosses a stream with a tiny waterfall on the right. It climbs high on the bluff a short distance, then follows the Poplar Spring Branch. After crossing the branch it drops back to Rock Creek. A stream flows through a pipe from the right, having traveled underground from a point 0.3 mi. upstream. The trail drops back to Rock Creek and crosses it, then follows an old railroad bed. After crossing the creek two more times, the trail reaches a white pine grove on the left, then ends at a forest road a short distance from Tenn. 154.

During a summer hike it is possible to cross Rock Creek and only wet the soles of your hiking boots. But the water is knee-deep during wet seasons. Also, there are icy spots on the trail in winter.

Fall Creek Falls State Park

This is a combination resort park and natural area, located on the western edge of the Cumberland Plateau between Spencer and Pikeville. It may be reached from Tenn. 30 (north entrance) or from Tenn. 111 (south entrance). The park, which straddles the Van Buren–Bledsoe county line, consists of 15,800 acres—land purchased by the National Park Service in 1935. Some development occurred during the Depression with the help of young men in the Civilian Conservation Corps (CCC) and others working under the Works Projects Administration (WPA). The land was deeded to the state of Tennessee for a park in 1944. The farms that were purchased by the National Park Service have reforested,

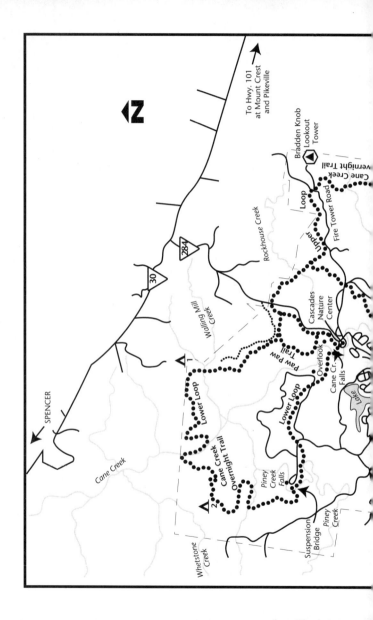

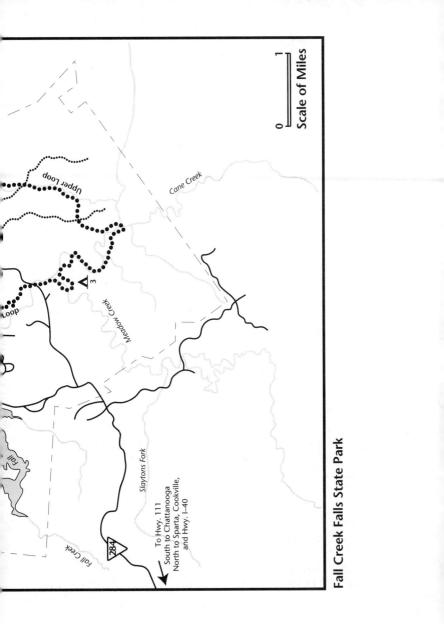

Fall Creek Falls State Park

mainly by natural succession, into almost pure stands of Virginia pine. The rest of the upland areas of the park are second growth oak-hickory forest, while the gorges are filled with stands of hemlock, basswood, yellow poplar, and yellow birch.

The major scenic attractions of the park are the gorges and their waterfalls. Fall Creek Falls, 256 ft. high, is 63 ft. higher than Niagara Falls. Views of the falls at the head of each gorge, as well as a broad overview of Cane Creek Gorge, are easily accessible by trail or by automobile. There are four short trails and two long overnight loops in the park. A trail map of the park is available for the asking from the Tennessee Department of Environment and Conservation, 7th Floor, L&C Tower, 401 Church Street, Nashville, TN 37243-0446. The map is a composite of appropriate topographic maps of the U.S. Geological Survey, reduced in size. The overnight trails and campsites are marked clearly in red and are accurately represented.

The short trails include the trail to the top of Fall Creek Falls, 1 mi. from the nature center to the top of the falls; the trail to the foot of Fall Creek Falls, 0.5 mi.; the Cable Trail to the foot of Cane Creek Falls, 0.2 mi.; and the Pawpaw Trail, a 4-mi. loop.

The Pawpaw Trail. Length, 4 mi.; rating, moderate. The trail, which is in a hardwood forest rich in wildflowers, leaves the parking lot of the nature center and parallels the road to the north entrance for several hundred yards. The Cable Trail to the foot of Cane Creek Falls leads off to the left 0.3 mi. from the nature center and descends abruptly 200 ft. to the bottom of the gorge. A few hundred yards farther along, a side trail exits to an east rim overlook of Cane Creek Falls. Shortly thereafter, the Pawpaw Trail begins a loop. The eastern side parallels the north entrance road to 1,800 ft. elevation. (The nature center is at 1,600 ft.) At the highest point on the loop, the Pawpaw Trail turns west for 0.5 mi., then south, roughly parallel to the eastern rim of the Cane Creek Gorge back to the beginning of the loop. One may return to the nature center by the connecting trail.

Overnight Trails. The two overnight trails are called the **Cane**

Creek Overnight Trail—Lower Loop (12 mi.) and the **Cane Creek Overnight Trail—Upper Loop** (13 mi.). Presumably, these designations refer to the lower and upper elevations of Cane Creek. The use of either trail requires registration at the nature center. A parking area is provided for users of the trails at the old Maintenance Center, 0.2 mi. south of the north entrance and 0.2 mi. east (left) of the main road. The parking area, on a trail that connects the two loops, is 0.3 mi. from the lower loop and 1 mi. from the upper loop. Each loop will be traversed in a clockwise direction with the center of each loop as a point of reference.

The Lower Loop encircles all of the gorges within the boundaries of the park. The trail dips into and crosses Cane Creek Gorge—an elevation change of 600 ft.—close to the northern boundary of the park. West of the parking area, the connector trail crosses the road from the north entrance and continues 100 yds. or so to the junction with the Pawpaw Trail. Either side of the Pawpaw Loop may be followed to the Nature Center. The Fall Creek Falls Trail is followed to the falls parking area, then the west road is taken for 25 to 50 yds. to a white blaze well up in the trees on the right. The trail leads to Piney Creek Falls (2 mi.) through rather open forest and glades where blueberries and wildflowers are abundant. An alternate route to Piney Creek Falls for those who like scenic overlooks (and don't mind sharing the road with automobiles) follows the Gorge Scenic Drive Motor Nature Trail (4 mi.). For this alternative, take the road north from the Fall Creek Falls parking area.

At Piney Creek there are rock ledges that serve as most satisfactory vantage points for observing the beauty of the falls and the upper end of Piney Creek Gorge. A suspension bridge crosses Piney Creek, and the next 2 miles are again on a gently rolling forest trail ending at campsite 2, as numbered by the Parks Division. The site is in a well-forested area, has three camping "nodes" that are placed to assure the privacy of each occupant, a privy, and a pump that produces clear, cold water. One-third of a mile past the campsite, the trail begins to descend into the gorge. For the most part the trail down is in good condition. However, some of the wooden footbridges may be slick in wet weather, and it is wise to be careful. In addition, there is a stretch of loose rocks where the footing may be insecure. Down in the gorge the vegetation becomes thicker, and at the edge of Cane Creek the trees and moss are thick and lush. From late fall to early spring, Cane Creek is a full, busy, and noisy stream. During all but the periods of highest flow, there are places to rock-hop across. By contrast, Cane Creek may become bone dry in summer. A bridge has been built at this point, providing a safer, more comfortable crossing when the creek is up.

Although water flows over the falls, it quickly disappears and flows underground. At the trail crossing one can usually find a pool within 200 to 300 yds. downstream, nestling in a desert of boulders. With luck, the water will be deep enough to submerge in and share a natural cooling system with timid minnows, crayfish, mayfly nymphs, and maybe even a very shy salamander. The trail out of the gorge follows a zigzag course up to the eastern rim. The 600 ft. of elevation that was lost in descending now has to be regained. If cool at the bottom, one is warm or even steaming by the time the top is reached. Fortunately, there are some outcrops on the way up that are rich in fossils, giving an excuse for a breather along the way. On the rim the trail again goes through gently rolling upland forest about 1 mi. to campsite 1. It is similar to campsite 2, but the water from the pump, while potable, is unusually rich in minerals. Two miles farther the trail returns to the maintenance center parking area via the north side of the Pawpaw Trail and the connector trail.

The Upper Loop is in the southern portion of the park and is entirely on the gently rolling upland plateau, average elevation 1,800 ft. The maximum variation in elevation along the trail is 200 ft. The southernmost tip of the loop comes within 0.7 mi. of the southern boundary of the park. The outstanding feature of this loop is the vegetation, with extensive fern beds sometimes covering several acres. Reforestation has been successful, and there is abundant animal life. Following the connector trail south, one comes to the beginning of the Upper Loop Trail within a short mile. Following the fork to the east (left), the trail reaches and crosses a gravel road after 1.5 mi. The road leads to the lookout tower on top of Bradden Knob, about 0.3 mi. off the trail. Bradden Knob is the highest point in the park, slightly more than 2,000 ft.

The trail goes almost due south for the next 3 mi. After a long mile the trail picks up Flatrock Branch and follows it to its confluence with Cane Creek, which it crosses on a suspension bridge. If it is a warm day, this is a good spot to take a swim—or a splash. Even when the creek below the falls is dry, this part usually has water flowing.

The eastern side of this loop has extensive fern beds and patches of blueberries. This part is hardly used, and ferns and other plants have grown in the trail. A wide variety of birds can be observed. On a July day a ruffed grouse and deer tracks may be seen in several areas. A mile past the suspension bridge, down Cane Creek, the trail reaches campsite 3. There are four camping nodes and a privy. The water supply comes from Cane Creek, which is no more than 30 yds. from any of the nodes. The water must be treated before drinking. Past campsite 3 the trail snakes along the Cane Creek bottoms for the next 1.5 mi., crossing Meadow Creek along the way; it crosses Cane Creek on an automobile bridge on one of the roads leading to the south entrance. Beyond the bridge and across the road, the trail enters woods again and ascends 100 ft. or so. After 3 mi. of forest and glades and one more road crossing, the trail reaches the connector trail to the maintenance center parking area.

The abundance of ferns and blueberries along the Upper Loop Trail suggests that an apt name might be the Fern-Blueberry Trail. The Lower Loop might be better named the Gorge Trail.

Standing Stone State Park

The park is located about 10 mi. southeast of Dale Hollow Dam on Tenn. 52. It is accessible from I-40, either via Tenn. 42 and 52 from

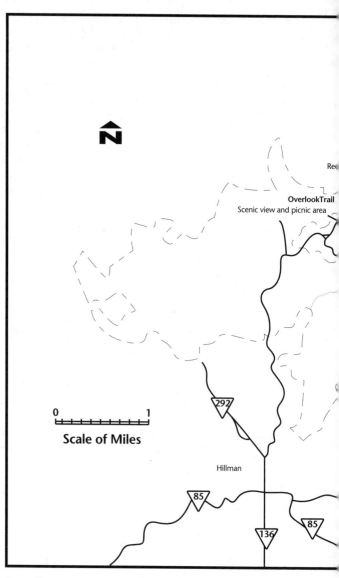

Standing Stone State Park

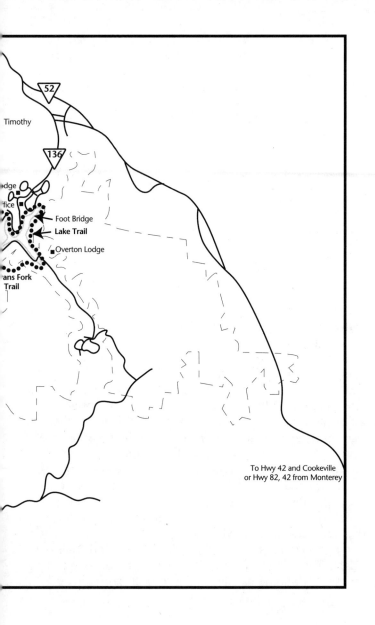

52

Timothy

136

dge

fice

Foot Bridge

Lake Trail

Overton Lodge

**ans Fork
Trail**

To Hwy 42 and Cookeville
or Hwy 82, 42 from Monterey

Cookeville or via Tenn. 84, 42, and 52 from Monterey. There are about 13 mi. of trails in the park and Standing Stone State Forest, but we like the diversity of the day loop described here.

Overlook, Bryan's Fork, Lake Trail Loop. Length, 5 mi.; rating, moderate. The loop may start and end at the swinging bridge below the dam, or an alternate loop may start from the park office parking area and end across the road from the recreation lodge. There are steep grades at both ends of the alternate route.

A steep switchback trail with guardrails leads down the bluff from the office area to the road along the lake. Turn right to a swinging bridge below the stone dam and cross to a trail junction. To the right, the trail goes over the hill to a picnic area and overlook. The left trail follows the lakeshore. The Overlook Trail, a steep switchback path to the top of the bluff, views the X-shaped lake. The trail veers to the left along the top of a narrow ridge, passing through a cedar glade at about 200 yds. from the top of the bluff, then follows an easy slope along the side of a ridge past a deformed tree on the right. The trail becomes steeper for 100 yds., rises briefly, and levels out again, veering back to the edge of the cliff in second-growth hardwoods. It now follows the top of a hill, crosses the head of a ravine, and goes through a stand of big beech trees to arrive at a road and a picnic area.

Crossing the road, the trail leaves the picnic area on a sharp right turn, following a hillside on a fairly level path. It crosses the head of a small ravine, and 100 yds. farther a bigger ravine, then curves left up an easy grade in open woods to the point of the bluff. Passing through an open area with heavy undergrowth, it starts downhill around the head of a ravine, then levels out briefly, following the contour. Descending, it follows the side of a steep hill, curves right, then sharply left across a steep ravine. Still downhill, the trail crosses one more ravine, near the bottom this time, and arrives at a creek and a paved road.

As one turns left across a wooden bridge, Bryan's Fork Trail is on the right. The trail crosses a thicket about 50 yds. wide and turns left along a hillside parallel to the road. It passes under a fallen beech tree at 100 yds., then crosses several fallen trees in open woods to a stand of big beech trees. Following an easy grade along the side of the hill for 0.2–0.5 mi., the trail curves right across the brow of a hill in upland hardwoods—hickory, oak, elm, and beech. The lake is now visible through the trees on the left. The trail curves right around the hill, slopes downward for 200 yds., then curves left around the head of a ravine and passes through a patch of crested dwarf iris. A series of switchbacks provides an easy grade to the bottom of the ravine, and the trail arrives at a road along the lakeshore (end of Bryan's Fork Trail).

Follow the road to the right to a bridge, cross it, and turn left to pick up the Lake Trail behind the Overton Lodge. The trail follows a long slope along the side of a bluff, with rock outcroppings on the right and the lake below on the left. There is treacherous footing crossing a ravine. Downhill briefly, the trail levels out again. A big rock is wedged between the small trees on the left. The trail now follows a ledge above the lakeshore and passes through a thicket at a ravine crossing, again with treacherous footing. It follows the bluff again, then swings right around the point of the next hill. At a footbridge there are two options: to follow the trail around the end of the lake or to cross and pick it up on the other side. If crossing the bridge, turn right a short distance to pick up the switchback trail up the side of the ravine to arrive at the Recreation Lodge. The other alternative continues around the lakeshore another 0.5 mi. to return to the swinging bridge below the dam.

Cedars of Lebanon State Park

This state park is east of Nashville and south of Lebanon, about 7 mi. south of I-40 on U.S. 231. It is one of the recreational areas along the Trail of Tears State Scenic Route, and it has unique features.

Hidden Springs Trail. Length, 4.5 mi.; rating, easy. The left fork at a Y intersection just beyond the park office leads to the parking area and the trailhead near the swimming pool. The 0.5-

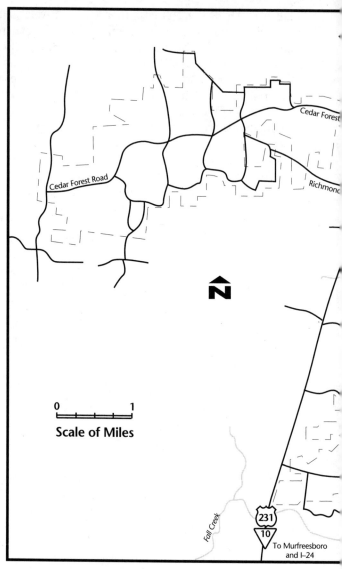

Cedar Forest

Cedar Forest Road

Richmond

N

0   1

Scale of Miles

Fall Creek

231

10

To Murfreesboro
and I–24

Cedars of Lebanon State Park

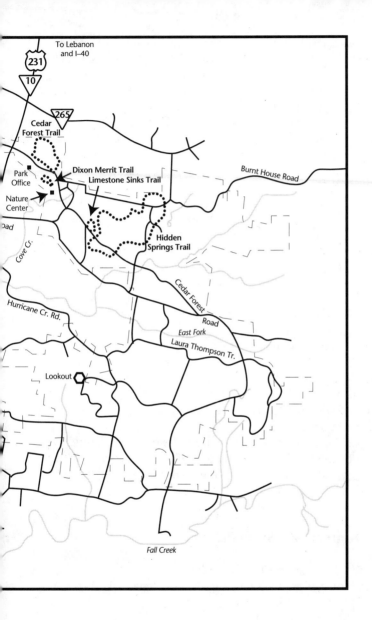

mi. Limestone Sinks Trail is also in this area. The trailhead of the 2-mi. Cedar Forest Trail is at the Y intersection. All are loop trails. Hidden Springs Trail is a day-use trail, with no camping allowed. Elevation changes are not great. Hours of operation are 8:00 a.m. to 10:00 p.m. in summer; 8:00 a.m. to 8:00 p.m. in winter.

The Hidden Springs Trail is a loop trail that meanders through cedar forests and glades past a broad array of unusual wildflowers and other native plants and trees. There limestone substrate underlying this area is known as karst topography, found also in the Karst Mountains of Slovenia and Croatia. The trail area is home for nineteen rare species of plants that grow only in middle-Tennessee cedar glades. There is the pink Tennessee cone flower that blooms early in summer. There are small annual herbs in the mustard family, such as the three species of glade cress with white or yellow flowers, and spring and early-blooming perennials such as the pale blue glade phlox on rocky outcrops. There are Tennessee milk-vetch with pale yellow flowers; purple glade violets; Gattinger's lobelia; the limestone fame flower; glade savory, a fragrant small mint; and the white-flowered sandwort.

Trees along the trail are shagbark hickory, eastern red cedar, fragrant sumac, honey locust, hackberry, and post oak. Near Hidden Spring on the right is a large limestone outcrop with an abundance of fossils. Hidden Spring Cave was once the location of a moonshine still, making use of the pure spring water and also the concealment of the cave.

Two old millstones are built into the stone wall behind the counter in the park office. There are no running streams in the park, but when the mill was running years ago the water to run it came from a large pond.

Montgomery Bell State Park

The park is 7 mi. east of Dickson on U.S. 70.

The Montgomery Bell Overnight Trail. Length, 11.7 mi.; rating, moderate; white blazes. This is a loop trail passing through a very historic and scenic area. From the park office, take the road fork toward the campground. Pass the campground entrance, cross the bridge, take the left road fork past the ranger's residence, and turn left to the parking area at the trailhead. From the trailhead go up the hill, cross the road, and continue on down to a small stream. About 50 yds. downstream are the remains of Laurel Furnace, which was built in 1815 to produce iron. This area contained the necessary ingredients—brown ore, limestone, and timber—for making charcoal. The trail goes uphill across the paved road on a section known as the Ore Pit Trail and soon comes to a small rest shelter. The left fork passes pits where ore was removed, primarily by slave labor. This ore, along with the charcoal and limestone, was removed from the hillside onto a wooden trestle and dumped into the top of the furnace.

The trail continues through this pit area to a point where it makes an abrupt turn to the left (south). A few feet north is one of the largest pits, which usually holds several feet of water. From here proceed down the hill to a log cabin, a replica of Samuel McAdow's home, where the Cumberland Presbyterian Church was organized in 1810. The trail goes west on an old road, crosses the stream twice, and bears south uphill to a rest shelter. Continue on to the entrance to Hall Cemetery, cross the entrance road through two gates, and continue south along the old roadbed. About ½ mile south the trail crosses Hall Creek and turns left down a slight hill to the Hall Spring campsite. Hall Spring emerges on the left, and the camping area is situated to the right.

The trail works its way downhill past another mine pit from which much of the sandstone was taken for construction of many of the buildings in the park. The trail then crosses the creek on a rustic bridge and continues through a marsh area to Hall Spring, which emerges from the large area on the right after crossing the next bridge. This is campsite 1, 3 mi. from the start; there is a shelter with eight bunks and a pit toilet. The water should be treated. From here the trail follows the stream, which harbors an active

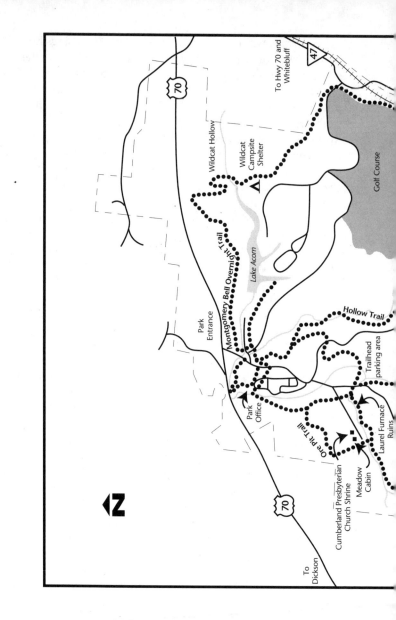

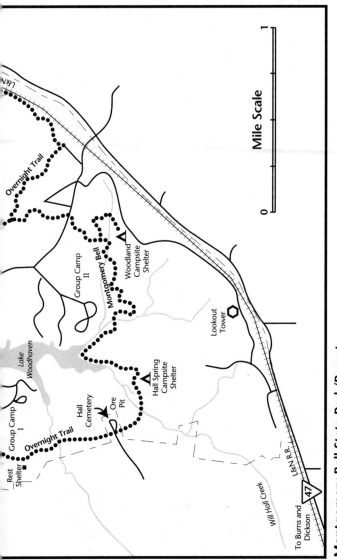

Montgomery Bell State Park/Resort

Mile Scale

0   1

TN 97

Overnight Trail

Group Camp II

Montgomery Bell

Woodland Campsite Shelter

Lake Woodhaven

Group Camp I

Rest Shelter

Overnight Trail

Hall Cemetery

Ore Pit

Hall Spring Campsite Shelter

Lookout Tower

Will Hall Creek

L&N R.R.

To Burns and Dickson

47

beaver colony. Jewelweed and cardinal flowers grow profusely here, along with several patches of cane.

If this area is approached quietly, there is a good chance to see beavers. Ducks and other wildlife also can usually be observed in this area. After the last beaver dam, the stream becomes Lake Woodhaven. There is a good view of the lake, then the trail turns right along the lakeshore for a short distance. Just before reaching a large oak log, the trail turns sharply to the right and continues through a hardwood forest into some nice areas of yellow pine. Shortly after crossing the third stream in this stretch, a spur trail to the right leads to campsite 2, known as Woodland, 4.7 mi. from the start. This campsite, which is 0.3 mi. off the main trail, has an eight-bunk shelter, pit toilet, and a good spring 50 yds. down the path in front of the shelter.

Back on the main trail, turn right uphill into a beautiful open upland forest. After crossing the paved road, the trail runs downhill to the upper end of Creech Hollow Lake, then bears right to a dirt road. Turn left and follow the road slightly more than a mile to the rear entrance to the park, then left on this road about 50 yds. to a sign indicating a right turn back into the forest. The trail follows the park boundary some distance and then descends to a small stream that leads to Wildcat Hollow, campsite 3, at 8.7 mi. The water supply—the stream—must be treated. This site is convenient for fishing, as Acorn Lake backs up to within a few yards.

The trail continues eastward across the creek in front of the shelter and along another stream for a short distance, then turns left across the stream and up the hill. At the crest of the hill, the trail bears left and soon becomes the roadbed that was once the old Nashville-Dickson highway. It is about 1 mi., mostly downhill, to the arts and crafts shop. Cross the bridge behind the shop and walk the paved road a short distance, and the trail picks up again opposite the playground. This section leads through another sandstone pit in which a beautiful grove of pine trees is now growing. There is a steep climb out of this pit, then the trail meanders through a mixed forest, crossing another paved road and off into a hollow. Eventually the trail winds down a stream that is crossed by a bridge just behind the park maintenance building. The trailhead parking area is in front of this building.

Nathan Bedford Forrest State Park

Located 8 mi. northeast of Camden on Kentucky Lake, the park may be reached from I-40 via U.S. 641 to Camden. Turn right on U.S. 70 and watch for the signs leading to the park.

This area is of unusual historical and geologic interest, being the site of a highly irregular conflict as well as containing the highest point of ground in West Tennessee. The Confederate attack on the Union redoubt and supply depot at Johnsonville, replaced by New Johnsonville since the construction of Kentucky Dam, not only was an easy victory for General Nathan Bedford Forrest but is also the only recorded instance in military annals of the defeat of a naval force by a cavalry regiment. Further details of the battle are available at park headquarters.

The park and most of the trail network lie along the wooded west bank of the Tennessee River (Kentucky Lake). It is an area of chert ridges and fertile valleys and abounds in a variety of hardwoods. Also found in abundance are many species of mosses, ferns, wildflowers, and shrubs. Mountain laurel adds its perpetual beauty to the higher ridges. A ranger-naturalist is in residence and is available for consultation. A campground with utility hookups is also available for the less hardy campers.

Three Mile Trail. Rating, moderate; yellow blazes. This is a loop trail that begins at the Tennessee River Folklife Center on Pilots Knob. It makes a gradual descent approximately 308 ft. into a hollow and follows the contour of the hollow to exit in a gradual climb to a ridge that leads back to the beginning.

Five Mile Trail. Rating, moderate; orange blazes. This trail covers most of the old Tennessee Forrest Trail that was sponsored by Boy Scout Troop 343 of Memphis, Tennessee, with patches and

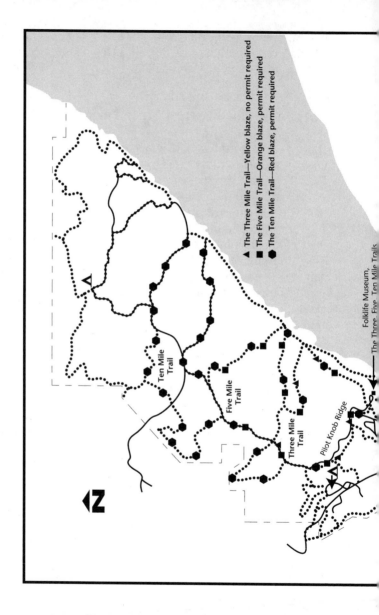

▲ The Three Mile Trail—Yellow blaze, no permit required

■ The Five Mile Trail—Orange blaze, permit required

⬟ The Ten Mile Trail— Red blaze, permit required

Ten Mile
Trail

Five Mile
Trail

Three Mile
Trail

Pilot Knob Ridge

Folklife Museum,
The Three Five Ten Mile Trails

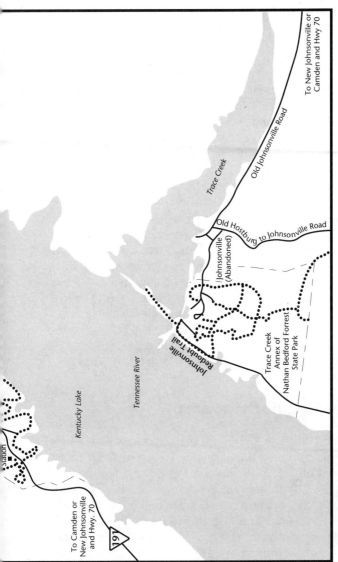

Nathan Bedford Forrest State Park

medals available for hikers. For further information regarding materials and patches, write to Ken Humphreys, P.O. Box 17507, Memphis, TN 38117.

Ten Mile Trail. Rating, moderate; red blazes. This trail also begins at the Folklife Center on Pilots Knob, but goes through more of the park. Hardwoods such as oak, hickory, yellow poplar, sycamore, river birch, beech, and cherry are in evidence. There are several varieties of fern and moss in the hollows along streams, and shrubs and wildflowers abound. Mountain laurel and flame azalea bloom in the spring. There are small mammals such as fox, raccoon, squirrel, as well as deer. Since the park is located near the Tennessee River Flyway, migrating ducks and geese may be seen in season. For brochures, maps, or information call (901) 584–6356 or write Nathan Bedford Forrest State Park, Eva, TN 38333.

Johnsonville Redoubt Trail. Length, approximately 4 mi.; rating, moderate. This trail is located in the Trace Creek Annex of Nathan Bedford Forrest State Park, across the Tennessee River from Pilot Knob. Access is from U.S. 70 in New Johnsonville, where a sign points north to the Johnsonville State Historic Area. The trail goes by sections of Old Johnsonville to historic sites such as redoubts, rifle pits, cemeteries, home sites, and the old railroad turnaround and railroad bed. For more information call (615) 535–2789 or write to Johnsonville State Historic Area, Denver, TN 37054.

Fort Pillow State Historical Area

Located on the Mississippi River at the first Chickasaw Bluff, this is where Fort Prud'homme was built by the French in 1682. To get there, turn west off U.S. 51, 9 mi. north of Covington near Henning on Tenn. 87. Trail maps are available at the visitor's center. There are picnic facilities and a good campground.

Fort Pillow Historical Trail. Length, 10 mi.; rating, moderate; maximum elevation change, 150 ft. For information about trail patches, contact Ken Humphreys, Historical Hiking Trails, Inc.,

P.O. Box 17507, Memphis, TN 38187. The trail starts on the road near the Inner Breastworks, elevation 400 ft. above mean sea level, and runs eastward a short distance before turning sharply to the north, following the breastworks past a 3-ft. post oak tree. Turning back to the west (left), the trail passes over several points of land believed to have been used by Confederate sharpshooters in the Battle of Fort Pillow, April 12, 1864. The trail crosses a ravine by way of a swinging bridge, then heads up the north slope past the area where the Union army occupied cabins, huts, and tents. It follows the bluff past the reconstructed main redoubt, which was held by Union troops. At the top of the hill there is a choice of routes.

Hikers taking the Historical Trek follow the yellow markers over another hill to reach a paved road, turn to the right, and hike southward 700 yds. past the road entering the park to reach the Outer Breastworks. The main trail follows the bluff to a path leading down the north face of the steep bluff, then turns west (left) to reach Cold Creek at the bottom. Here hikers have the choice of following Cold Creek to the right to reach the paved road or taking the Ravine Alternate, which is more interesting and challenging during dry weather. This route is blazed in red. It leads back around the west and south sides of the hill on which the main redoubt is located, turns left, and follows a marked path eastward on higher ground to the road. The trail follows the road along the creek on the right, then leaves the road in the area where the Outer Breastworks approached the river; it goes east and south, then west past the remnants of the Outer Breastworks.

After crossing the road again, the trail follows the main east-west portion of the Outer Breastworks for about 1.5 mi. to Fort Pillow Lake. There is a beaver dam on the left below the dam that forms the lake. Crossing the dam and following the road uphill to the northwest, there are more breastworks parallel to the road on the left. The trail turns left through a break in the breastworks and follows a ridge, then drops into a low area above the beaver pond, elevation 270 ft. Now it goes up a steep hill to the top of a ridge, elevation about 380 ft., and follows the top of the ridge to the

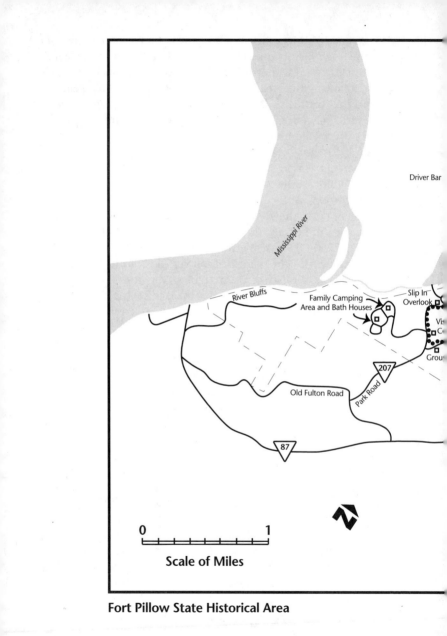

Fort Pillow State Historical Area

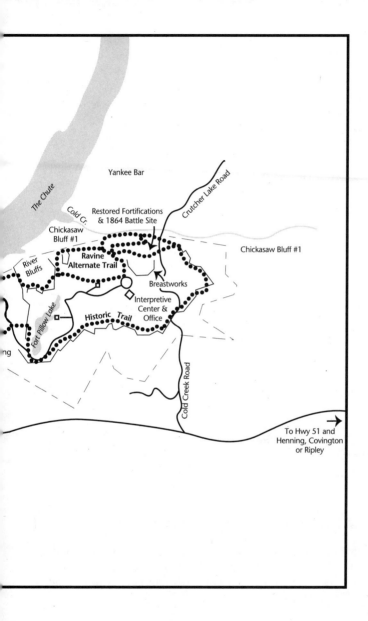

Yankee Bar

The Chute

Cold Cr

Crutcher Lake Road

Restored Fortifications
& 1864 Battle Site

Chickasaw
Bluff #1

Chickasaw Bluff #1

River
Bluffs

**Ravine
Alternate Trail**

Breastworks

Fort Pillow Lake

Interpretive
Center &
Office

Historic   Trail

ng

Cold Creek Road

To Hwy 51 and
Henning, Covington
or Ripley

road. Here the trail turns right and follows the road about 0.5 mi. to the Slip In observation point. This is the upper end of the first Chickasaw Bluff, which "slipped in" to the Mississippi River in 1907, blocking the Cold Creek Chute. The elevation is about 420 ft., and the river is at 210 ft. An industrial plant is visible on the Arkansas side of the Mississippi River immediately upstream, and Osceola, Arkansas, 7 mi. upriver to the northwest, can be seen on a clear day. There is a picnic area at the observation point.

Again, the trail follows the road downhill around a U-turn and leaves the road, turning right. It now goes uphill to the northwest to the top of a bluff, then northward to the west leg of the Outer Breastworks, turning east along more breastworks, which were the connecting link between the outer works and the inner fortified hills. The trail now descends to a dirt road, goes left about 400 ft., then north (right) up the side of one of the fortified hills along more breastworks. It goes left to the edge of the bluff, parallels the edge for a short distance, passes the end of more breastworks, and travels downhill to another dirt road. The trail follows the road a short way, then turns left up the next hill and follows more breast-works around the top of the hill to the edge of the bluff. It runs east along the bluff, then downhill and generally eastward to a point overlooking the ravine that was crossed on the first leg of the trip. From here the trail runs south, ascending a steep, wooded ridge to another section of the Inner Breastworks, and follows it to the starting point.

Two other trails are the Fort Pillow Historical Trek, 5-mi. loop suitable for younger hikers; and the one-way First Chickasaw Bluff Trail, 5 mi., which has an adequate campsite 1 mi. from the south end. All three Fort Pillow trails have nice patch awards.

Meeman-Shelby Forest Day Use Park

The park is on the third Chickasaw Bluff, 13 mi. north of Memphis. To get there, go north on North Watkins Street from either I-240 or U.S. 51 and watch for the signs. The route is well marked from the end of North Watkins. There are about 11 mi. of hiking trails in the park, plus a 5-mile bicycle path. The trails have been "adopted" by the Memphis Chapter of the Tennessee Trails Association. The Tennessee Department of Conservation built 6 mi. of the Chickasaw Bluffs State Scenic Trail in 1976. The terrain is hilly, interlaced with small streams and forested with huge bottomland hardwood trees.

Chickasaw Bluffs Trail. Length, 8 mi.; rating, easy to moderate. The trailhead, with a nearby parking lot, is at the north end of the park, just east of the Mississippi River Group Camp. Trail, blazed in white, begins at the top of a ridge, descends steeply, and follows a horsetail-lined stream, crossing it several times. The group cabins are on a hill to the west; high, erosive bluffs are to the east. In between is thick hardwood forest. Beware of newly fallen trees which may obstruct the trail.

After crossing a road, pick up the trail a short distance to your right. For a long stretch the trail is straight and level, surrounded by beech trees. Continue along the left edge of an open field, with the wildlife management area on your right. Cross the old road bridge, which is closed to vehicles. Trail leaves the roadbed to the left and continues on a slight rise, never more than 100 ft. from the road. It rejoins the road briefly, then reenters the forest and meets the Woodland Trail Juncture (blazed in red). The trail ascends steeply to Woodland Trail Shelter.

After leaving the shelter, cross the end of a paved road and pick up the trail just to the right of the bike path. It now converges with the Pioneer Springs Trail, blazed in blue. After twisting and turning, climbing a ridge and descending, the trail crosses a gravel road and levels off, paralleling the bike trail, which is just a few yards to the left. Trail narrows as it bisects a dense horsetail thicket. A short distance farther, look on your left for the tree growing through the roof of an ancient rusty car.

The bluffs on the left become higher, while on your right are swampy bottomlands filled with cypress "knees." (Mosquito repellent here is imperative.) The trail passes around the makeshift shel-

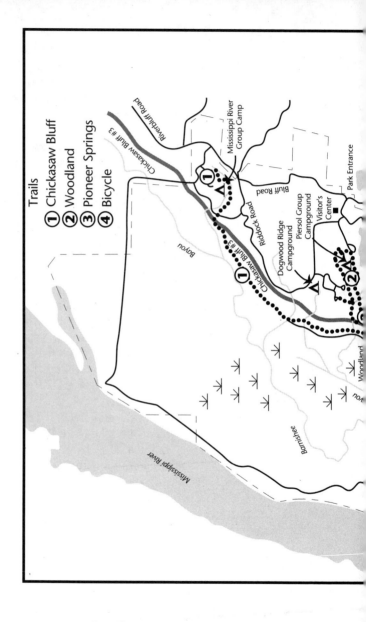

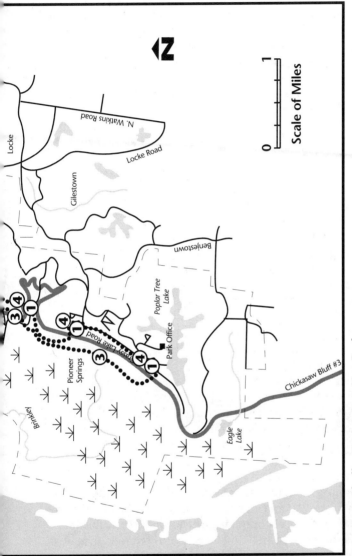

Meeman-Shelby Forest Day Use Park

Scale of Miles

0   1

ter over Pioneer Springs. Observe—but don't drink—the water as it bubbles up from the sand. The 1½ mi. of trail from here to Poplar Tree Lake are heavily used. A very steep hill leads up to the terminus at the lake parking lot.

Woodland Trail. Length, 3 miles; rating, easy to moderate. This is a loop trail, blazed in red, that begins and ends at the park's nature museum. It starts as a straight path along a ridge heading west, then descends to the left down "steps" formed by tree roots. At the bottom of this hill, you have a choice: go to the right for a short one-mile loop, or go left, cross the bridge, and climb a steep hill for the full 3 miles. On this route, the trail will pass a precipitous sheer bluff and turn left, meandering through beautiful forestland (look for beds of trillium in April). The trail crosses a stream (with no bridge), climbs another steep hill, and turns right. After leveling off briefly, it descends to the stream, turns left, rises and falls, crosses a bridge, climbs again.

Here you will meet up with another arm of the trail, also blazed in red. Turn left and look for a 2-foot-high post painted red. From this point, if you go south, you'll emerge on an old road that is now part of the bike path. If you continue west, you'll meet up with the Chickasaw Bluffs Trail (blazed in white) and follow it up to the Woodland Trail Shelter, which has benches for eating lunch but is not designed for camping.

Returning from the shelter to the juncture point, take the western leg of the trail, which, in contrast to the first half, is almost completely level. Go down to the stream and cross it to the left (no bridge). Look for the stands of bamboo, and for the pileated woodpeckers that live in the trees here. About halfway back, there is a trail spur to your left that reaches the Dogwood Ridge campground in 0.8 miles.

Continuing straight, the trail generally follows the stream, eventually crossing it and climbing a hill back to the museum. An interpretive brochure about the plants encountered on this trail is available at the park office (901–876–5215), as is a topo map of all the trails in the park.

6. Other State Trails

South Cumberland State Recreation Area

This is a system of natural areas, day-use areas, and other private and public lands in Grundy, Marion, and Franklin counties, linked together by highways and trails. It includes the Savage Gulf, Grundy Forest, Carter, Hawkins Cove, and Sewanee Natural Bridge State natural areas; the Grundy Lakes and Visitor Center day-use areas; and the Foster Falls and Little Gizzard Creek TVA small wild areas. Also within the system is the Fiery Gizzard State Recreation Trail, which runs mostly across private lands to link the Grundy Forest, Foster Falls, and Little Gizzard Creek areas.

Fiery Gizzard Trail. Length, 13 mi.; rating, moderate to difficult. This is an overnight backpacking trail with sections that make excellent day trips, located in Grundy and Marion counties. The Grundy County trailhead is in the Grundy Forest Natural Area, 6 mi. from I-24 at Monteagle and 1 mi. off Tenn. 56 in Tracy City. The Marion County trailhead is in the Foster Falls Small Wild Area off U.S. Hwy. 41, 7 mi. southeast of Tracy City and 7 mi. north of Jasper.

The trail is named for Fiery Gizzard Creek and Cove, which it follows. The name is said to have come from a story about Davy Crockett burning his tongue on a hot turkey gizzard while camping in the area, but there are other stories just as interesting. The trail is well known for spectacular scenery that includes waterfalls, deep gorges, sheer rock bluffs, scenic overlooks, spring wildflowers, exceptional fall colors, and dazzling ice formations in winter.

Starting at Grundy Forest, the trail soon descends into the gorge and continues in it until the 500-ft. ascent to Raven Point in the fifth mile. This section is exceptionally spectacular but very difficult. The huge trees, rock formations, waterfalls, and cool swimming holes are well worth the struggle across the millions of rocks.

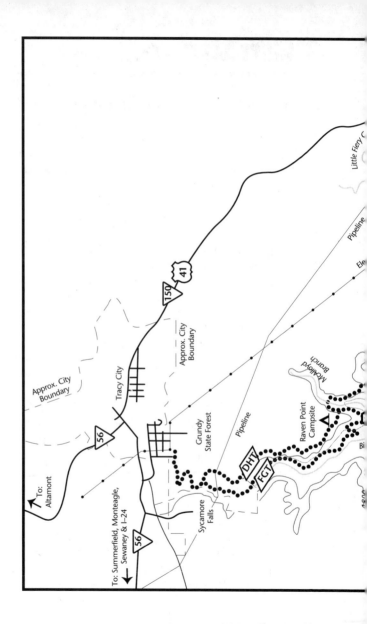

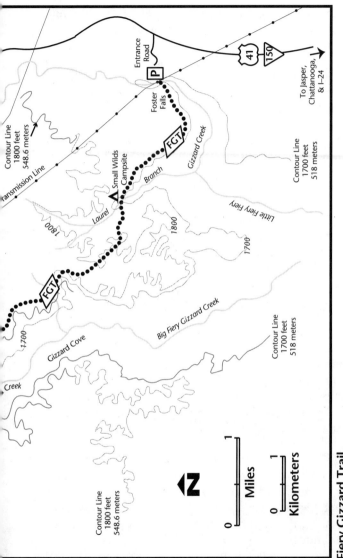

Fiery Gizzard Trail

There is a campsite on the plateau near Raven Point, but no campfires are allowed. A spur trail leads to the Raven Point Overlook, one of the most beautiful views of the plateau.

The Dog Hole Trail. Length, 2.8 mi. This new trail leads from the campsite back along the north rim of the gorge and down into Grundy Forest to rejoin the main trail near Sycamore Falls. This is a nice trail with overlooks and other points of interest, offering an easier way to Raven Point and the possibility of walking a loop. The Marion County section begins at Raven Point and runs mostly along the top of the plateau on its way to Foster Falls. The first mile is great, with a nice overlook and crossings of two beautiful streams. The next 3 mi. cut across a recently logged tableland. Abruptly the Laurel Branch Gorge is crossed at mile 4. This rugged gorge is one of the trail's most scenic features.

Soon after the Laurel Branch crossing, there is a campsite that, with the gorge below it, makes up the Little Gizzard Creek Small Wild Area. Campfires are allowed in the small wild areas. The last 2.5 mi. to Foster Falls have some of the best views on the trail as it runs along the edge of the escarpment above Little Gizzard Creek, ending at the gorgeous falls. Water can be scarce along the Fiery Gizzard, so it is advisable to carry a canteen. Water from the main stream is unsafe for consumption. Camping is restricted to the two campsites mentioned above.

Buggytop Trail. Length, 2 mi.; rating, difficult. This trail provides the only public access to the Carter State Natural Area. The trailhead and parking area are on Tenn. 56 between Sewanee and Sherwood, about 10 mi. south of I-24 at Monteagle. This trail leads to the Buggytop entrance of the Lost Cove Cave. Thomas Barr wrote in *Caves of Tennessee* that Buggytop is "one of the most impressive cave openings in the state." At the base of a 150-ft. limestone cliff, a beautiful cascading creek flows from the opening, which is 80 ft. high and 100 ft. wide. Exploration of the cave is allowed, but taking the monthly guided tour is a good way to get oriented for future trips on your own.

The trail crosses Saddle Mountain to reach the cave. The first section is a rocky climb to the top of the ridge. Then a fairly easy half mile along the crest of the ridge brings you to the sign-up booth where the trail map is displayed. This ridge, known as "The Spur," has several wildflowers in season, including the rare Cumberland Rosinweed which blooms in late summer. Just beyond the sign-up booth, the trail descends to the old Lost Cove Road (abandoned) and the clifftop above the cave. Turning right, the trail drops steeply to the cave mouth. This short descent makes the 4-mi. round trip worthwhile because it's simply spectacular.

Stone Door Trail. Length, 1 mi.; rating, easy. The trail starts at the Stone Door ranger station, the western entrance to the Savage Gulf State Natural Area. The trailhead is reached from Tenn. 56 at Beersheba Springs, 25 mi. north of Monteagle and 20 mi. south of McMinnville. This trail is easy, with wide tread and gentle slopes that persons with handicaps can negotiate in wheelchairs. The Stone Door Overlook, at 1,800 ft. elevation, provides a breathtaking view of the 800-ft.-deep Big Creek Gulf. The cliffs are popular with rockclimbers and rappellers.

The "Great Stone Door," a crevice in the bluff, provided a passage onto the plateau for the Chickamauga Trace Indian Trail.

Big Creek Gulf Trail. Length, 4 mi.; rating, difficult. This trail connects the Stone Door with Alum Gap. It runs through the "gulf" (gorge), making it a very strenuous trail. The exceptional scenery along this trail includes towering sandstone cliffs, giant boulders, the tumbling crystalline waters of Big Creek, and some extraordinary geological phenomena. At the halfway point, a half-mile spur trail leads to Ranger Creek Falls, a 30-ft. waterfall that drops over and disappears under the same limestone bluff. Directly below the Stone Door, a number of springs bring the water back to the surface after a 2-mi. underground stretch. The sink that swallows Big Creek is 0.75 mi. past the Ranger Falls spur, just off the trail. Upstream from the sink, the stream flows in its boulder-strewn bed most of the year. This is one of the most interesting trails in the state.

Big Creek Rim Trail. Length, 3.2 mi.; rating, easy. The trail

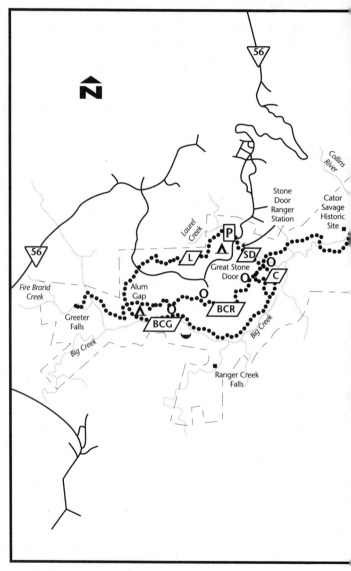

**South Cumberland State Recreation Area
(Savage Gulf State Natural Area)**

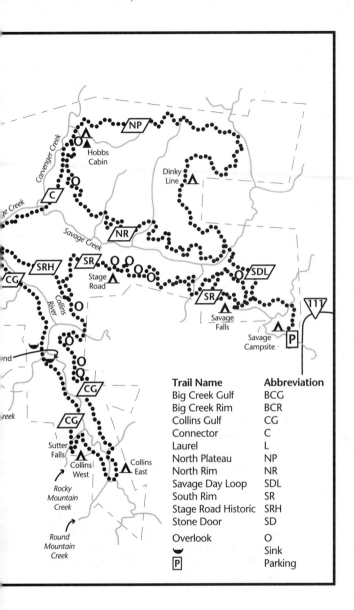

Trail Name	Abbreviation
Big Creek Gulf	BCG
Big Creek Rim	BCR
Collins Gulf	CG
Connector	C
Laurel	L
North Plateau	NP
North Rim	NR
Savage Day Loop	SDL
South Rim	SR
Stage Road Historic	SRH
Stone Door	SD
Overlook	O
◡	Sink
P	Parking

connects Stone Door with Alum Gap campsite. Together with the Big Creek Gulf or Laurel Trails, this is a great trail for a long, interesting day hike or short overnight trip. The trail follows the blufftops with four major overlooks and gently rolling terrain.

Laurel Trail. Length, 2.9 mi.; rating, easy. The trail begins directly behind the Stone Door ranger station and runs to the Alum Gap campsite. The trail crosses numerous moist, fern-filled hollows where a rare white orchid is found sometimes. This trail makes a great return from either Big Creek trail and is the shortest way to the back country campsite.

The Connector Trail. Length, 6.7 mi.; rating, difficult. It connects all the Savage Gulf Natural Area trail system. It is all in the gulf and crosses seemingly endless rocky slopes. Although it crosses Big Creek, Collins River, and Savage Creek, there is usually no need to worry about getting wet unless there have been unusually heavy rains. The major streams are forded downstream from the sinks that swallow the entire flow 99 percent of the time. There is a pioneer cabin between the Big Creek and Collins River crossings at the Cator-Savage Historic Site. There is a campsite at the halfway point, directly across from the Collins Gulf Trail junction.

Collins Gulf Trail. Length, 10 mi.; rating, difficult. The trail runs along the rim to a junction with the South Rim Trail and the Stagecoach Road at the top of Peak Mountain, along a line of cliffs in the middle of the view from the Stone Door. The Collins East campsite is located near the descent into the gulf, where the trail crosses the Collins River on house-size boulders. From there it stays in the gulf. A mile from the boulder crossing, Rocky Point is visible above the trail. A spur trail leads up to Collins West campsite and a view of the falls and cliffs of Rocky Mountain Creek. The trail follows the wall of a cliff below an imposing overhang with a series of three waterfalls below. Fording Rocky Mountain Creek, the trail descends to the bottom of the gulf where the Collins River plunges over Pound Falls and disappears into a sink. Horsepound (or Pound) Gulf was the site of a "pound" where stolen livestock were kept during the Civil War. Local guerrilla groups with no fixed allegiance to the South or North stole indiscriminately from both sides. The remoteness and inaccessibility of the gulf made it ideal as both a hideout and a cache for plunder. The largest tributary gulf, Fall Creek, enters below Pound Falls but disappears into a sink before it reaches the trail. There is little water, but great scenery, from here to the junction with the Connector Trail.

The Stagecoach Trail. Length, 1.5 mi.; rating, moderate. The trail is a section of the Chattanooga to McMinnville Stage Road, built mostly by slave labor in 1836. It runs from the Connector Trail up Peak Mountain to the junction of the South Rim and Collins Gulf trails. Near the top there are extraordinary stone walls built by the slaves. This trail is on the National Register of Historic Places.

South Rim Trail. Length, 6 mi.; rating, moderate. The trail follows the south rim of Savage Gulf. It starts from the Savage Day Loop, crosses to the south side of Savage Creek on a suspension bridge, and follows the creek down to Savage Falls. The Savage Falls campsite is at the top of the hill just beyond the falls. The trail follows the rim 4.5 mi., passing spur trails leading to overlooks, a moonshine still site, and several old-growth trees. The Stage Road campsite is at mile 5, after which the trail crosses Peak Mountain to the junction with the Collins Gulf and Stagecoach trails.

North Rim Trail. Length, 6.3 mi.; rating, moderate. Perhaps the most spectacular trail in the Savage Gulf Natural area, it starts on the back side of the Savage Day Loop and crosses the picturesque Meadow Creek. A half mile past the creek is Meadow Creek Bluff, the first of many striking overlooks. The overlooks get more and more spectacular as the gulf gets wider and deeper. Unlike the South Rim, these views are very near or right on the trail. At an overlook called Tommy Point, one can see the gulf mouth, Peak Mountain, and, in the distance, the Stone Door cliffs. From Tommy Point, the trail turns north and follows the rim of Coppinger Creek, to Hobbs Cabin, where there are a log trail shelter and wonderful pine woods campsites. The junction of the North Rim, Connector, and North Plateau trails is near Hobbs Cabin.

North Plateau Trail. Length, 7 mi.; rating, easy. This trail crosses the plateau north of Savage Gulf, where stately old-growth shortleaf pines tower over the forest. Although generally flat, it crosses the line of hills known as Cagle Knobs. The hollow on the east side of Cagle Knobs contains an outstanding old-growth hardwood forest. The Dinky Line Campsite is 1.5 mi. from the North Rim Trail at Meadow Creek. This section follows the bed of a narrow-gauge logging railroad operated by the Werner Family in the 1920s. The gulf was never logged, while the north plateau was sparsely logged, and the state acquired it in 1973 to preserve the big timber.

Savage Day Loop Trail. Length, 2 mi.; rating, easy. This trail provides access to all the other Savage Gulf trails from the Savage Gulf ranger station, 6 mi. north of Palmer on Tenn. 399. It has a great overlook of Savage Falls and a grand view down the gulf from Rattlesnake Point. On the back side of the loop is a beautiful old-growth hardwood stand. Pink lady's slipper orchids and mountain laurel decorate the trail in May, along with many other flowers. The first mile is also the last mile, with the actual loop being 2 mi. long. The South Rim Trail starts between the loop junction and the Savage Falls Overlook, and the North Rim Trail starts between Rattlesnake Point and the Loop junction.

Lone Rock Trail. This is a short trail at Grundy Lakes State Park. The Grundy Lakes site was a coal-mining and convict labor operation in the late 1800s, and several historic ruins of mines, buildings, and (most interestingly) the 136 coke ovens are visible along the trail. The whole site is listed on the National Historic Register.

Big Hill Pond State Park

The park, originally developed as Big Hill Pond Environmental Education Area, is southwest of Shiloh near the Mississippi state line. Its variety of terrain and ecosystems, from river bottom marshes to dry rocky ridgetops, makes for interesting hiking, birding, and botanizing. It has more than 25 mi. of foot trails with four trail shelters, affording a number of attractive loop options for day hikers or weekend backpackers. It may be reached from U.S. 45, 8 mi. south of Selmer, via Tenn. 57 west through Ramer and south at the sign for the park. It is 3.2 mi. to the entrance to park headquarters on the right. The Southern Railroad crosses the area, running northwest to southeast, 0.6 mi. from the entrance. Much of the work was done by Comprehensive Employment Training (CETA) workers and the YCC. U.S.G.S. quad sheet Chewalla 4SW includes this area.

Big Hill Pond Trail. Length, 4.8 mi.; rating, moderate. This trail begins on John Howell Road about 0.5 mi. south of the park office. It meanders southward through rolling and steep hills, then swings westward around and down the hillside above the old Big Hill Pond. Turning northward it follows the edge of the marsh and ascends to the head of the hollow above the pond. Climbing out the west side of the hollow and paralleling John Howell Road, it soon meets the Azalea Spring Day Loop, and together the trails cross the road, go north a short distance, and part. The Big Hill Pond Trail first goes east, gradually turning northward, then proceeds along the contour 80 to 100 feet above the east side of Travis McNatt Lake until it crosses a hollow and makes a steep final climb to a trail intersection at the ridgetop. A left turn leads down to a footbridge across an arm of the lake and on to the boat dock or picnic area. A right turn leads 0.3 mi. back to the original trailhead.

Azalea Spring Day Loop. Length, 2.6 mi.; rating, moderate. This trail starts on John Howell Road about 2 mi. south of the park office. Coincident with the Big Hill Pond Trail, it goes north a short distance then leaves the latter and heads northwest to round the point at the south end of Travis McNatt Lake. Rounding the next hollow it descends toward the dam, rounds the point above it, and swings southward to follow the edge of Dismal Swamp (Tennessee has one, too) to the Southern Railroad. It follows the rail line a scant 0.5 mi. before turning north, climbing to the ridgetop, and following it back to the trailhead. Along this trail is a severely burned area with a section demonstrating prime reforestation.

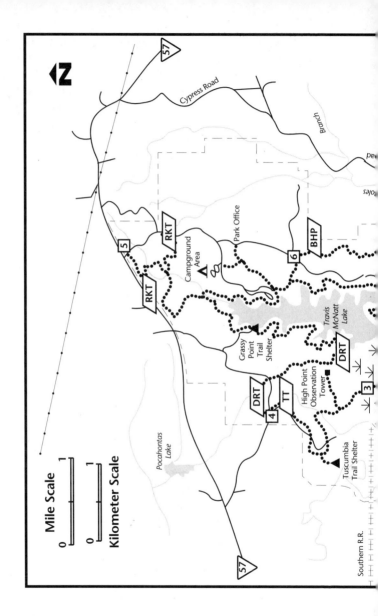

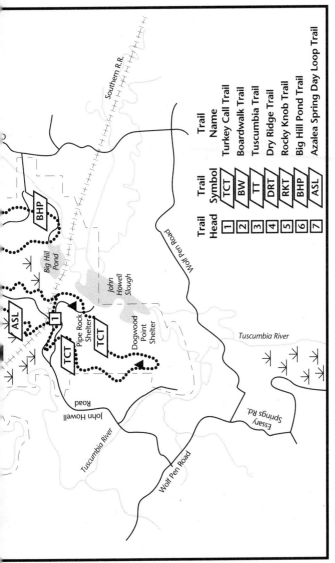

Trail Head	Trail Symbol	Trail Name
1	TCT	Turkey Call Trail
2	BW	Boardwalk Trail
3	TT	Tuscumbia Trail
4	DRT	Dry Ridge Trail
5	RKT	Rocky Knob Trail
6	BHP	Big Hill Pond Trail
7	ASL	Azalea Spring Day Loop Trail

Big Hill Pond State Park

Turkey Call Trail. Length, 3.8 mi.; rating, moderate. This trail begins at the intersection of John Howell Road and the Southern Railroad. It heads east coinciding with the Azalea Spring Day Loop for about 0.2 mi., then south to the Pipe Rock Shelter side trail. Continuing generally southeast along the edge of John Howell Slough, it crosses several small watercourses, then goes south at the foot of a long ridge. Just past an ox-bow in the slough, the trail turns sharply north to climb the steep southern end of the ridge among interesting rock outcroppings approaching Dogwood Point Shelter. It then follows the crest of the ridge between Tuscumbia River and Cypress Creek for almost 2 mi. back to the point of origin.

Boardwalk. Length, 0.8 mi.; rating, easy. This boardwalk connects Azalea Spring Day Loop with the Tuscumbia Trail. It crosses Dismal Swamp, a unique area with abundant wildlife.

Tuscumbia Trail. Length, 1.3 mi.; rating, moderate. This section of trail is probably the most scenic on Big Hill Pond State Park; it offers many vistas along the rim of the Tuscumbia River Bottom. Along the trail is a 75-foot observation tower and Tuscumbia Trail Shelter. It connects the Boardwalk Trail with the Dry Ridge Trail.

Dry Ridge Trail. Length, 7.5 mi.; rating, moderate. From its intersection with the Tuscumbia Trail, this trail circles along the crest of a horseshoe-shaped ridge to the northeast, then east, then south. Rounding a high point above the lower end of Travis McNatt Lake, it follows the west side of the lake northeastward, crossing several small watercourses and passing Grassy Point trail shelter and an old cattle dipping vat (circa 1930). Well upstream of the lake, it crosses Dismal Branch and follows the east side of the valley south to the boat dock and picnic area.

Rocky Knob Trail. Length, 0.6 mi.; rating, moderate. Starting on John Howell Road just inside the park entrance, a short section of the trail climbs to the top of the knob just east of the road. Starting at this trailhead most of the trail winds west of the road through this area, unique for its large boulders and rock outcrops, and returns to the road about 0.3 mi. southeast of the trailhead.

Midway along this loop a connector trail, less than 1 mi. in length, branches off to the right, leading first west then south to the northernmost point of the Dry Ridge Trail.

Herb Parsons Lake

Fisherville Nature Trail. Length, approximately 7 mi.; rating, easy. This trail is located in Fayette County at Herb Parsons Lake on land managed by Tennessee Wildlife Resources Agency (TWRA). It was originally established and maintained by Boy Scouts of America; however, BSA no longer does this. The Memphis Chapter of Tennessee Trails Association recently blazed and cleared the trail. There are no maps available. From Memphis go east on Highway 57 (Poplar Avenue) through Collierville, Tennessee. Turn north (left) on Collierville-Arlington Road and stay on this road until you come to Monterey. Turn east (right) on Monterey to Fisherville Road where there will be a sign directing you to Herb Parsons Lake. Turn left and go a short distance to the lake entrance on your right.

Begin the hike by walking in a southerly direction across the dam and following the trail into a grove of pine trees. The trail basically follows the contours of the lake. There are some low areas and creeks through which the trail passes, and it can be wet at certain times of the year. A bridge has been built over the main creek, and the lake is being kept lower than usual, which helps control some of the marshy areas. Along the way you can see loblolly pines and hardwoods such as oak, hickory, dogwood, maple, and river birch. There are turtles, snakes, frogs, and fish in the lake. You can also spot mallards, Canada geese, great blue herons, and an occasional egret. A good variety of raptors, songbirds, small animals, and occasional deer can be seen.

The first 4 miles of trail will end at Lakeview Road. Turn left on Lakeview Road, go a short distance, and turn left again into the woods to complete the last 3 miles of trail. This last section is sometimes used by bow hunters, and there will be a TWRA sign here informing you of this. Hikers should check with the lake office to see when the bow hunters will be having a meet. If they are, you have two choices: You can retrace your steps or continue down Lakeview Road in a northwesterly direction to Fisherville Road. Turn left here and this will bring you back to the lake office, a distance of 1 mile. If you need further information, the lake-office phone number is (901) 853–0751, or contact: Memphis Chapter TTA, 2995 Carvel, Memphis, TN 38118.

7. Historical Trails

Cumberland Gap

Here is one of the most significant and scenic spots in Tennessee history. Through it, for centuries, the Warrior's Path linked the tribes of the midwest with those of the southeast, and in the late 1700s the Wilderness Road was the major route for settlers coming from Virginia and North Carolina into Kentucky and middle Tennessee. During the Civil War it was held by each side for a time and extensively fortified against an invasion that never came.

Cumberland Gap National Historical Park contains more than 20,000 acres in Kentucky, Virginia, and Tennessee. It encompasses roughly 20 miles of the northeast-southwest ridge called Cumberland Mountain, with the Gap crossing near the lower end of this tract. There are more than 50 miles of hiking trails in the park including the 17-mile Ridge Trail from the pinnacle on the northeast side of the Gap to the White Rocks overlooking Ewing, Virginia. U.S. 25E passes through the Gap and near the park visitor center at Middlesboro, Kentucky. The Gap itself lies between Kentucky and Virginia, but just below it, at the southeast foot of the mountain, the historic town of Cumberland Gap lies in Tennessee.

By 1996 a four-lane tunnel will open a new highway route beneath the mountain, and the Cumberland Gap will be restored to its late-1700s setting. It will then become the main trailhead for the park and will connect the Ridge Trail with the Tri-State Trail. Presently under study is a proposed conversion into a hike/bike trail of an abandoned railroad from Cumberland Gap, Tennessee, up Powell Valley through Ewing, Virginia. Completion of this project would provide a superbly scenic 30-mile ridge and valley loop trail between the Cumberland Gap trailhead and the White Rocks near the northern end of the Ridge Trail.

Wilderness Road Trail. Length, 3.5 miles; rating, moderate.

The trail begins near the Iron Furnace in Cumberland Gap, Tennessee, and follows a path close to the original Wilderness Road. After passing through the saddle of the Gap, it meets the Tri-State Trail, which it follows to the Fort Foote side trail. Here it starts down the mountain to end near the Pinnacle Road 0.4 miles from the park visitor center.

Tri-State Trail. Length 0.9 miles; rating, moderate. This trail begins at the parking area on U.S. 25E just below the saddle of the Gap on the Kentucky side. This is also the trailhead for section 1 of the Cumberland State Scenic Trail, which here coincides with the Tri-State Trail. After meeting the Wilderness Road Trail 0.1 mile above the parking area, it passes a Civil War commissary and magazine site, then turns up the mountain to the point on the crest where Kentucky, Tennessee, and Virginia meet, marked by a small shelter with informative plaques. From this point a side trail continues 0.5 mile along the crest to Fort Farragut, a Civil War artillery emplacement. The Cumberland State Scenic Trail continues from here to the southwest.

For further information, write Cumberland Gap National Historical Park, P.O. Box 1848, Middlesboro, KY 40965-1848.

Lookout Mountain

This spot, in Chickamauga and Chattanooga National Military Park, is steeped in history. The national park and an adjoining tract called Reflection Riding have been the scene of many historic events. De Soto followed the Great Indian Warpath through this area in 1540. It overlooks the sites of the upper Chickamauga towns wiped out in 1779 by Virginia militia under Col. Evan Shelby and, again, in 1782 by forces under "Nolichucky Jack" Sevier. The five lower Chickamauga towns lay just west of Lookout Mountain, and two of these were destroyed in 1794 by a force of Kentucky and Tennessee volunteers under Maj. James Ore. Then there was the famous "Battle Above the Clouds" in 1863. Famous landmarks include Sunset Rock, Point Park, Cravens House, and the "Castle in the Sky," a former resort hotel now occupied by Covenant College. There are more than 30 mi. of trails in the park, all built by the CCC between 1934 and 1940. U.S.G.S. quads: Chattanooga, 105SE, and Fort Oglethorpe, 106NE.

Bluff Trail. Length, 4.5 mi.; rating, moderate. Many trails branch off and are well marked. The hike spreads from Point Park to Covenant College. From Point Park the trail is reached by metal steps to the left of Ochs Museum. Here the Kentucky Volunteers climbed the mountain to plant their flag after the Battle Above the Clouds; there is a view that commands the broad curves of Moccasin Bend, Signal Mountain, and Missionary Ridge. The first 0.5 mi. of trail gradually descends, following the bed of a narrow-gauge railroad called the Dinky Line. At the junction of the Cravens House Trail to the right, it follows the 1,800-ft. contour, more or less, and Sunset Rock looms into view 0.7 mi. farther. Confederate General Longstreet stood here to direct operations during the struggle for Lookout Mountain. Nowadays, people come here to rappel, to hawk-watch, to watch the hang gliders floating down from Raccoon Mountain, or just to sit and look at the distant Cumberlands or peaceful Lookout Valley.

The trail is good hiking any time of the year. In winter the icicles hanging from the rocky bluffs make for a photographer's paradise. Wildflowers, shrubs, and ferns are in masses, and lichens cover dripping rocks. The rock formations are extremely interesting, with cavelike openings, overhangs, and several spots where it is not hard to visualize an Indian with a campfire. There is beautiful Skyuka Spring (not recommended for drinking—foot dipping, yes). Metal walkways span slides and areas where it was impossible to carve out a trail from the bluff, and there are natural benches along the way for resting. At the Jackson Gap Trail junction, veer left and make a 300-ft. climb to the Covenant College parking area. Cars could be parked at Covenant College; at Ochs Gateway; at Sunset Rock, where there is a walkway up to a parking area on West Brow Road; or at Point Park.

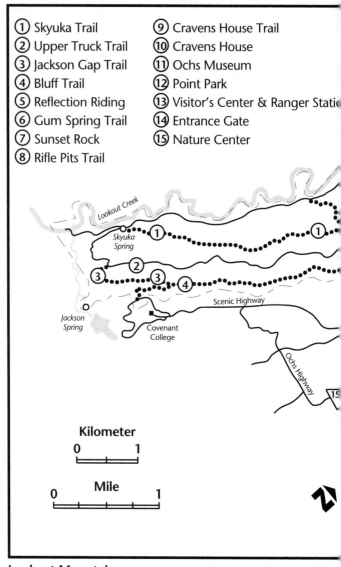

1. Skyuka Trail
2. Upper Truck Trail
3. Jackson Gap Trail
4. Bluff Trail
5. Reflection Riding
6. Gum Spring Trail
7. Sunset Rock
8. Rifle Pits Trail
9. Cravens House Trail
10. Cravens House
11. Ochs Museum
12. Point Park
13. Visitor's Center & Ranger Station
14. Entrance Gate
15. Nature Center

Lookout Creek

Skyuka Spring

Jackson Spring

Covenant College

Scenic Highway

Ochs Highway

Kilometer

0   1

Mile

0   1

Lookout Mountain—
Chickamauga & Chattanooga National Military Park

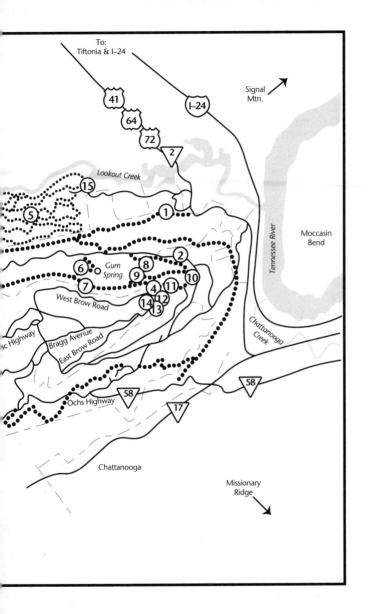

Skyuka Spring Trail. Length, 7.7 mi.; rating, moderate. Covenant College to Tenn. Hwy. 318. It would be well to start this hike at Covenant College, as there is a mountainside descent of 2.8 mi. to the Skyuka Spring. Turn left at the junction of this access trail with the Bluff Trail and then veer right where the Jackson Gap Trail joins the Bluff Trail. The access trail is highlighted by rock formations, laurel, rhododendrons, ferns, numerous varieties of trees, and a view of Lookout Valley all the way down. The trail is so constructed that the elevation drop of 1,800 ft. does not seem difficult. Skyuka Spring is named for the Indian Chief Skyuka, whose village was located here. Overnight camping is permitted, but a special permit must be obtained at the headquarters at Point Park; fires are not allowed. The spring water runs into Lookout Creek close by.

A short distance after leaving Skyuka, there is a fork in the trail and Skyuka Trail bears right. The left fork is a service road that follows the creek into Reflection Riding. This can also be hiked as part of the Scouts' Blue Beaver Trail. This name was taken from the "Beavers in Blue," a phrase coined by the Confederates to describe the activity of the Union soldiers bottled up in Chattanooga in 1863. They were said to be always clearing trees—for fuel, shelter, and fortification. On leaving the spring there is a gradual climb to the 900-ft. level; the trail seems to maintain this elevation (more or less) until nearing the end.

Autumn is the most satisfying time of the year to hike the Skyuka, as the 5.5 mi. from the spring to the trail's end is under a canopy of trees, mainly hardwoods. All vie to put forth their brightest reds and yellows with just enough green to contrast. There are many rock outcroppings with interesting erosion patterns. There is a gradual descent near the end on Tenn. 318, a spur off U.S. 64. Cars can be parked at a nearby restaurant.

Cravens House, Bluff, Gum Springs Trail Loop. Length, 4 mi.; rating, easy. The trail begins at Cravens House, the home of Robert Cravens. The original house, used by generals of both armies, was destroyed in the Battle Above the Clouds and was rebuilt by Cravens in 1866. At the junction with the Bluff Trail, stay to the left and continue past the steps to Sunset Rock to the marker pointing to Gum Spring, 1 mi. to the right. There is a steep but not too difficult descent of 300 ft.

The Gum Spring Trail dead-ends into the Upper Truck Trail; turn right and follow what seems to be a tree tunnel where bird life abounds. This is really a National Park Service road and is also used as a horse trail. After less than a mile of easy walking, there is an option of continuing on the Upper Truck Trail to Cravens House or making a right turn to return on the Rifle Pits Trail. Along the Rifle Pits Trail there are rock circles and a wall that were no doubt used by the Confederates in battle. Some archaeologists say the origin of these stone structures goes back to the woodland culture, a prehistoric period. It is just 0.5 mi. back to Cravens House—a hike of natural, historical, and archaeological interest.

The Blue Beaver Trail and the Nolichucky Jack Trail are Scout Award Trails administered by Blue Beaver Trail, Inc., P.O. Box 38, Hixson, TN 37343. They follow generally the trails described in this chapter. Additional information may be obtained by writing to the above address.

Natchez Trace National Scenic Trail

The Natchez Trace is one of the best-remembered landmarks from the era of United States expansion into the Old Southwest. For over two decades in the early 1800s, it was the most significant highway in this region and one of the most important in the nation. In places, the Tennessee segment of the Natchez Trace National Scenic Trail follows sections of the original Trace and passes several sites of historical significance.

The southern trailhead lies about a quarter mile northeast of the site of John Gordon's ferry on the Duck River. Gordon, first postmaster in Nashville, began operating the ferry in 1802. A few hundred yards east of the ferry crossing is Gordon's restored home built in 1817–18, mostly under the supervision of his wife while he was away serving as a scout with General Andrew Jackson.

A few miles northeast of Duck River, beside a narrow section of the old Trace still used as a county road, is the now overgrown site of a hand-dug well where Andrew Jackson is said to have stopped on his many trips along the Trace. Local legend has it that two men who operated a stand (inn) here were killed by robbers.

At the Tennessee Valley Divide parking area, the trail crosses Duck River Ridge which was, until at least 1805, the eastern boundary of Chickasaw territory. About 2.5 miles to the north, the trail tops out on Butler Ridge at the Old Trace parking area. Captain (later Colonel) Thomas Butler was one of two U.S. Army officers who led troops working on the trace in the 1801–3 period. The last 1.7 miles of the trail to Garrison Creek, the northern trailhead, follow Butler Ridge on the longest remaining unimproved section of the Natchez Trace in Tennessee. Garrison Creek was named for a nearby U.S. Army post here in 1801–2.

The Tennessee segment of the National Scenic Trail traverses one of the hilliest parts of the Old Trace route and provides some of its best vistas. The Water Valley Overlook across the Parkway from the trail at milepost 411.8 and the overlook at the end of the short spur trail above the Garrison Creek parking area offer particularly rewarding views of wooded hills and pastoral valleys at any time of the year.

This rolling terrain and variety of habitats support a wide diversity of native flora and fauna. White-tailed deer and wild turkey can be spotted anywhere on the trail, and red-tailed hawks and barred owls are often heard or seen. Also heard or seen in the appropriate habitat along the trail, and at the appropriate time of year, are at least fifty other species of breeding birds. The 1.5-mile section between the Tennessee Valley Divide and the Burns Branch parking areas is especially rich in its variety of hardwood trees and shrubs, flowering plants, and ferns.

Natchez Trace National Scenic Trail. Length, 24.5 mi.; rating, moderate; use, hiking and horseback

Parkway Milepost	Access Points	Trail Miles
427.6	Garrison Creek Parking Area* (staging area and northern terminus of trail)	0.0
426.2	Old Trace Parking Area	2.1
425.2	Burns Branch Parking Area	1.3
423.8	Tennessee Valley Divide Parking Area	1.4
422.9	Carter Road Staging Area (no parkway access)	1.2
415.6	Highway 7 Staging Area (access via Highway 7 and county road on northeast side of parkway)	8.9
408	Highway 50 Staging Area* (southern terminus of trail) Access via Highway 50 and Totty Lane along west side of parkway)	9.6
		24.5

*Comfort stations and drinking water available.

Fort Henry Hiking Trails

These trails are located in Land Between the Lakes, between Kentucky and Barkley lakes in Tennessee and Kentucky. This 26-mi. system of interconnecting loops closely follows the route of General U.S. Grant's troops in his campaign to capture Fort Donelson during the Civil War. The system starts at the parking lot off Fort Henry-Blue Springs Road (clearly marked by highway signs) and ends at the South Welcome Station on the Trace. Signs along the way describe military actions that took place at these points. In addition to the historical resource, the Fort Henry Trails traverse a variety of hardwood and pine forests along ridges and bottomlands where deer and turkey sightings are common. Located in the Tennessee portion of the Land Between the Lakes, this 170,000-acre recreation and environmental education area is operated by the Tennessee Valley Authority. TVA-LBL personnel were assisted by college students, historians, the National Park Service, and two scout troops—Dover Troop 501 and Clarksville Troop 314—in developing this trail system. Trail markings are located at each trail junction and on trailside trees.

The system, which became a national recreation trail in October 1976, is designed so hikers can plan an hour hike or an overnight trip. Camping must be off the marked trails; campfires are permitted except in the periods of high fire danger. The Piney Campground, with full facilities, is nearby, and there are numerous primitive campgrounds in the area. Hikers must register at either end of the Telegraph Trail, which runs from the South Information Center on Tenn. 49 (known as "The Trace") to Fort Henry parallel to Blue Spring Road. Trail maps are available at the South Welcome Station and at Piney Campground. Other trails in the system include Peyton, Tennessee Ridge, Artillery, Devil's Backbone, Piney, Shortleaf Pine, Telegraph Pickett, Pickett Loop, and Boswell.

Shiloh Military Trails

This system of hikes is sponsored by Shiloh Military Trails, Inc., P.O. Box 17507, Memphis, Tennessee 38187, and approved by the Boy Scouts of America. The trails mostly follow roadways in Shiloh National Military Park, the scene of one of the bloodiest battles of the Civil War. The park is located 7 mi. south of U.S. 64 on Tenn. 22 or 14 mi. east of U.S. 45, south of Selmer on Tenn. 142. There are eleven patch award hikes, including military, historical, environmental, and compass cross-country. Of these, nine range from 10 to 20 miles in length, are rated easy, and are recommended for Scouts 11 years old and up. Two are for younger hikers: the 2-mi. Shiloh Battlefield Trail and the 3-mi. Shiloh Indian Mound Trail. Maps and required reading material may be ordered from the above address. For information call Ken Humphreys, person-to-person, at (901) 323–2739. If no answer, call or write Trail Headquarters, Troop 343 Scout Hut, Kingsway Christian Church, 6310 Poplar Avenue, Memphis, TN 38119, phone (901) 681–0058 (person-to-person).

8. Trails on Federal Land

Tennessee Valley Authority Small Wild Areas

The TVA has set aside fifteen tracts of land to be preserved as small wild areas. Two are on the Cumberland Plateau, and the rest are on TVA reservoir land. They vary in size from eight to 300 acres, and each contains unique natural features, such as caves, waterfalls, and springs. Trails were developed by YCC and YACC crews, and there are five national recreation trails in these areas. The River Bluff Trail on the Norris Dam Reservation was dedicated as a national recreation trail on June 10, 1976. The Lady Finger Bluff Trail on Kentucky Lake received state and national recreation trail designation on April 13, 1978. The Hemlock Bluff Trail was designated a national recreation trail on Nov. 27, 1981. We describe these three trails and TVA's newest small wild area and trail here.

Hemlock Bluff National Recreation Trail. Length, 6.5 mi.; rating, moderate. This trail, entirely on TVA property, provides a scenic hike along steep ridges and bluffs with numerous views of Norris Lake. The trailhead, with three parking spaces, is located in Union County, Tennessee, at the Loyston Point Recreation Area, on the road to the boat ramp. Loyston Point also has a campground, picnic area, and swimming beach.

From the parking area the trail briefly descends, then climbs through a hardwood forest and soon crosses a gravel road (closed to traffic). It is a good idea to note this intersection, since this road is part of the return trip. After passing the road, the trail descends through hardwood and pine forests and reaches the lake edge after about 0.5 mi. The trail immediately climbs steeply to a ridge, levels out on a contour, and then climbs again to a ridgetop at about 1 mi. from the trailhead.

The trail descends steeply from the ridge, then turns sharply and follows the lake edge along a small embayment. A wildlife food plot is visible to the right of the sharp turn. This point is about 1.5 mi. from the trailhead. The terrain becomes less steep as the trail follows the lake edge for about 1 mi. When the terrain again becomes steeper, the trail begins a series of switchbacks up to a high ridgetop. The ridgetop is about 3 mi. from the trailhead. The trail follows the ridgetop, and after about another 0.5 mi., the first hemlocks become visible to the left. The small grove of hemlocks, which gives the trail its name, is visible on both sides of the trail for several hundred yards. At 4 mi. from the trailhead, the trail descends through a pine forest. At 4½ mi., the trail passes old homesites along an old road in a grove of cedar and pine trees, then passes rock outcrops. At 5 mi., the trail descends into a small gully and makes a sharp turn at the end of it. It then ascends to a gravel road.

Continue by turning right on the gravel-and-grass road, which passes wildlife openings and food plots. After about a mile, the road climbs to a hilltop. When reaching the hilltop, start looking for the trail crossing while walking along the ridge. Turn left to return to the parking area for a total hike of about 6½ mi.

River Bluff Trail. Length, 3.1 mi.; rating, easy. To get there take the first left turn off U.S. 441 after passing the overlook across the Norris Dam from the visitor's center. The road will fork immediately. Take the left fork down the hill to the parking area at the trailhead, elevation 1,000 ft. This loop trail passes through three distinct forest regions. From the parking lot, the trail first passes through a pine plantation that was decimated by southern pine bark beetles in the 1970s. This area is characterized by young dogwoods, redbuds, American beech, and maple. Pine trees killed by southern pine bark beetles are slowly decomposing into the soil and providing nutrients for successional hardwoods. Take the left fork of the trail, descending gradually toward the Clinch River at 840 ft.

The lower part of the trail near the river is famous for wildflowers in the spring. In April, yellow adder's tongue (also called trout lily), trillium, bloodroot, twinleaf, and toothwort bloom in profusion along with a few bright yellow celandine poppies. Ferns grow in the shade of a towering limestone bluff on the right, and equisetum (also called scouring rush) grows along the riverbank on the left. Canada geese are often seen and heard in this section of the river. Trout fishermen in waders ply their skills in the river during low flows. Near Hibbs Island and the low water dam (also called a weir), the trail begins a long gradual climb. Dutchman's breeches, phlox, and twin leaf are prominent spring wildflowers in this section of the trail.

The upper region of the area is drier, less protected, and usually warmer than the lower part of the trail. Squaw root, ginger, toothworts, and mayapples are found on these drier sites. Near the top, 1,100 ft. elevation, the trail passes an old chestnut tree trunk, all that remains of a noble giant that was stricken by the blight of the 1920s. A bench provides opportunity to enjoy a moment of solitude and to catch your breath. The trail levels out and follows the crest of the ridge. Tulip poplars have reached tremendous size and age here. Many show signs of lightning strikes and have broken tops. They provide cavities and roosts for owls, woodpeckers, flying squirrels, and raccoons. The descent back to the original trail passes through some remaining Chinese chestnut trees that were planted for wildlife mast after the American chestnut blight.

Flower patterns change with the seasons, from the yellow and white of spring flowers to the blue and purple of asters and Joe Pye weed in the fall. You can hike the River Bluff Trail over and over and always find something new. A free brochure and spring wildflower key is available by writing TVA, Wildlife and Natural Heritage Resources Section, Norris, TN 37828.

Big Ridge Trail. Length, 1.3 mi.; rating, easy to moderate. Not to be confused with Big Ridge State Park. This area is near Chattanooga, Tennessee. Take State Highway 153 north across Chickamauga Dam. Take the first right after crossing the dam. Take the first left onto Lake Resort Drive. Take the first left into the North Chickamauga Creek Greenway. Walk the paved greenway beside North Chickamauga Creek. At ½ mile the Big Ridge Trail turns off into the woods at the trailhead sign. The first part of the trail is an old woods road that led to a homesite at the top of the ridge. The trail follows a gentle grade through second growth hardwood forest of chestnut oak, red oak, hickory, and persimmon. It turns left when it reaches the ridge and continues along the ridge with backward views of Chickamauga reservoir and Chickamauga dam. The homesite is visible as a patchy clearing on top of the ridge. All that remains are a stone cistern and June blooming day lillies. The trail meanders through the woods on top of the ridge and enters an old growth forest as it begins the downhill section of the loop. Some of the trees in this section are estimated at 200 years old. Note the thick loose soil underfoot that characterizes these undisturbed forests. Largest trees in this section include tulip poplar, white oak, American beech, sugar and red maples, sassafras, and buckeye. Early spring wildflowers are false Solomon's seal, Solomon's seal, toothwort, spring beauty, larkspur, trillium, bellwort, doll's eyes, and bloodroot. This section of the trail generally follows the contour and returns to the main trail. Turn right and in a few hundred yards you will be back on the greenway.

This trail was constructed by two Boy Scouts as Eagle Award projects and is maintained by Boy Scout Troop 223. The 207 area TVA Small Wild Area has been designated an urban wildlife sanctuary by the National Institute for Urban Wildlife.

Lady Finger Bluff Trail. Length, 2.5 mi.; rating, moderate. This trail lies in the small wild area of the same name at the mouth of the Lick Creek enbayment of Kentucky Lake. To get there, turn right (north) off Tenn. 200-100 at Linden, then take 90 left on Lick Creek Road 8 mi. and follow the signs. This was Tennessee's twelfth national recreation trail and the nation's 115th. From the parking area the trail winds around the head of a small cove, crossing the inlet on a footbridge, then traveling over a low hill to the main shoreline near water level through hardwood timber. Spring flowers along the trail include blue phlox, star grass, wood sorrel, shooting star, and red trillium. On dedication day, April 13, 1978, a jack-in-the-pulpit had pushed through the trail tread at one point. The trail curves right to follow the main body of the lake a short distance, swinging right up Stocking Hollow, named for a narrow embayment shaped like the foot and ankle of a stocking. It curves left around the "heel" and follows the shoreline to the head of the embayment, then turns left across a footbridge and turns back left uphill.

Climbing a sharp rise on native stone steps, the trail reaches a fork, the beginning and end of a loop over Lady Finger Bluff, shaped like a lady's finger. It curves right at the top to follow the edge of the bluff northward about 200 ft. above the surface of the Tennessee River, the "narrows" of Kentucky Lake. A section of the Tennessee National Wildlife Refuge lies across the river. There are several vantage points for views of the lake and the surrounding countryside. Skeletons of gnarled cedars, resembling the famous bristlecone pines of the West, stand at the edge of the bluff. After 0.3 mi. the trail curves right again and runs back downhill to the end of the loop, backtracking to the trailhead. A free brochure is available by writing TVA as noted above.

Obed Wild and Scenic River

Added to the National Park System by Congress in 1976, sections of four streams course within this watershed. Cutting deeply into the sandstone of the Cumberland Plateau, the Obed and its tributaries have carved spectacular gorges as much as 500 ft. deep, dotted with huge boulders and rimmed by overhanging bluffs. With its variety of slopes and aspects, the area supports a rich diversity of plants and animals and a mixture of forest types.

Much of the river system flows through Catoosa Wildlife Management Area under State jurisdiction. It provides habitat for more than one hundred breeding bird species, including the rare red-cockaded woodpecker, as well as bobcat, mink, fox, and whitetail deer. The clear swift water supports populations of bass, muskellunge, bluegill, and catfish. The Catoosa Area is a favorite of deer, turkey, and small game hunters during managed hunts and/or open seasons. Obed River, Daddy's Creek, and Clear Creek are popular with experienced white-water canoeists and kayakers.

Hiking opportunities within the Obed Wild and Scenic River area are presently offered mostly by old logging roads in Catoosa Wildlife Management Area except during hunting seasons. The General Management Plan for Obed Wild and Scenic River calls for development of a trail system. The options among routes and trail-use possibilities—hiking, horse, mountain bike, motorized—are under study. Proposals should be ready shortly for public hearings. It is likely that phased development of the system, with much reliance on private volunteers, will be proposed. A first step might be a 2 mi., or so, trail from a new overlook (recently funded) at Lilly bridge along the south rim of Clear Creek gorge to an overlook above the junction of Clear Creek and the Obed. The next phase might be a loop of 20+ mi. up the north rim of the Obed from Clear Creek, then north across Catoosa (and private land to be acquired) to the south rim of Clear Creek at Barnett bridge and back down Clear Creek to Lilly bridge. Another future possibility is a trail of 20+ mi. along the south rim of the Obed from Nemo Bridge to the Devils Breakfast Table (here coincident with the proposed route for Section 4 of the Cumberland State Scenic Trail) and on to Adams bridge. The first 2 mi. of this trail has been developed. The Obed Wild and Scenic River Visitor Center is in Wartburg on U.S. 27, 22 mi. north of I-40. For information write: Manager, Obed Wild and Scenic River, P.O. Box 429, Wartburg, TN 37887; Manager, Catoosa Wildlife Management Area, 216 East Penfield, Crossville, TN 38555.

Nemo Trail. Length, 2.0 mi.; rating, moderate. This trail begins at a parking area on the west side of the Emory River at Nemo bridge. The bridge is located on Catoosa Road about 6.0 mi. southwest of Wartburg. The trail was built by T.V.A. in the mid-1980s. It leads upstream along the river's left bank, gradually working its way up to the bluffline and following along the top of the bluffs on the south side of Obed River until it enters an old logging road and descends to the Obed at Alley Ford. It features interesting geological formations along the bluffs, winter glimpses of the Obed, and an abandoned coal mine well into the process of reclamation by nature.

Big South Fork National River and Recreation Area

This 105,000-acre mostly forested preserve lies about two-thirds in Tennessee and one-third in Kentucky, along the north-flowing Big South Fork of the Cumberland River. It was set aside for outdoor recreation focused on the river system and its deep rugged gorges. Besides the sheer scenic beauty of its seemingly endless cliffs and rock houses, natural arches, and waterfalls, it is a prime locale for white-water canoeing and rafting, fishing and hunting, and horse-back and mountain bike riding. There are also over 200 miles of trails reserved exclusively for hikers. The Bandy Creek Campground and Visitor Center is located on Bandy Creek Road off Tennessee 297 about 12 miles west of Oneida.

Twin Arches Loop Trail. Length, 5.9 miles; rating, difficult. From Bandy Creek Visitor Center go west on Tennessee 297 to Tennessee 154, turn right, and go 1.8 miles on Tennessee 154. Turn right onto Divide Road and go 1.3 miles to a fork. Take left fork, Divide Road, for another 2.7 miles to another fork. Take right fork, Twin Arches Road, and follow it 2.4 miles to the Twin Arches trailhead.

Twin Arches is one of the most popular destinations in B.S.F.N.R.A., and the loop trail also passes a primitive campsite at an old abandoned farmstead and Charit Creek Lodge, a hostel for backpackers and horse trail riders. From the trailhead the Twin Arches Trail leads 0.7 mile out a narrow ridge, down two sets of steep stairs, and along the base of the bluff to the North Arch.

The Twin Arches Loop Trail passes under the North Arch (93-ft. span, 51-ft. clearance) and travels just over 1.5 mile, first along the bluff line past several huge rock shelters, then descending to Station Camp Creek. Here a field, a lone chimney, a spring, and a nearby cemetery mark the site of a pioneer farm of the 1800s abandoned in the 1930s. Proceeding down Station Camp Creek almost a mile, the trail joins a gravel road and quickly reaches a bridge over Charit Creek, with Charit Creek Lodge just beyond. The original building underlying part of this structure may date back to the early 1800s, and the site itself is reputed to have been a station camp of "long hunters" in the 1760s. The long hunters were skilled woodsmen and marksmen, mostly from Virginia and North Carolina, who came across the mountains in small groups on horseback and spent many months at a time (sometimes more than a year) exploring the Cumberland River watershed. Finding an area they liked, they set up a station camp and hunted until the game became scarce or until enough animal pelts had been collected to make the return from their "long hunt" profitable.

From the lodge the trail ascends steeply 1.1 mile back to the base of the arches. From here a short trail to the left leads under the South Arch (135-ft. span, 70-ft. clearance); a stairway between arches leads to the top of the bluff and back across the top of the North Arch; while the Twin Arches Loop Trail continues ¼ mile to the right back to the North Arch where the Twin Arches Trail returns 0.7 mile to the trailhead.

Honey Creek Loop Trail. Length, 5 mi.; rating, difficult. Turn west off U.S. 27 onto Tenn. 52 at Elgin, then right at a pocket-wilderness sign, less than 0.5 mi. from U.S. 27. Follow a paved county road about 3.5 mi. to a four-way intersection, continue straight ahead 0.5 mi. to a fork, and bear left to shortly reach Burnt Mill Bridge. Cross the bridge and continue about 3.5 mi. to the Honey Creek parking area on the right.

One of the most beautiful of the B.S.F.N.R.A. trails on a yard-by-yard basis, this rugged little 5.6-mi. loop trail on the Big South Fork of the Cumberland River does not have the large, spectacular attractions of some of the other trails. It does have much to offer, however: a number of small waterfalls, intriguing rock formations, rock houses used by Indians for temporary shelter during hunting trips, massive boulders jumbled in creek beds, and a wide variety

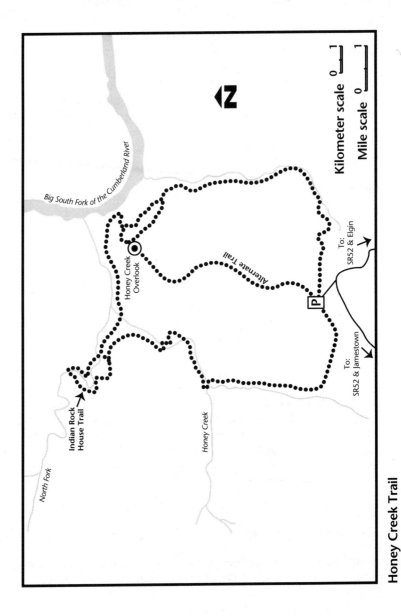

Honey Creek Trail

of Cumberland Plateau vegetation. The trail follows natural gorges around a small mesa of managed timberland and is an excellent example of what can be done with a relatively small amount of land with proper study and usage. Most of the trail lies within a block of 109 acres originally set aside as a Bowater Pocket Wilderness; yet the feeling of isolation is virtually complete once the hiker leaves the road and parking area. Note: This is the most rugged of all the trails covered while doing research for this guidebook.

Honey Creek Overlook provides a spectacular view of the Big South Fork from a vantage point some 250 ft. above the river. This point may be reached by a shorter walk down an old woods road designated as an alternate trail. A gate across this road is kept locked to prevent abuse and overuse of a very fragile area.

The Sheltowee Trace National Recreation Trail. Length, about 260 miles; rating, moderate to difficult. It starts at the Hidden Passage Trailhead in Pickett State Park and coincides with the first 5 miles of that trail and with the first 9.5 miles of the John Muir Trail. (The John Muir Trail, 90% of which is in B.S.F.N.R.A., is described in chapters 3 and 4.) The John Muir Trail branches off to the right about a mile before the Sheltowee Trace leaves B.S.F.N.R.A. to enter Daniel Boone National Forest in Kentucky. From here the trace continues 59 miles to Cumberland Falls State Park and almost 200 miles farther northeast to end near the Licking River in Cowan County, Kentucky. Much of the Trace north of Cumberland Falls lies on roads, and some of it is open to horseback and off-road vehicle use. Extended hikes on the Sheltowee Trace should be carefully planned only after receiving up-to-date information from the U.S. Forest Service, Stearns Ranger District, P.O. Box 429, Whitley City, KY 42653 and from Big South Fork National Recreation Area, P.O. Box 630, Oneida, TN 37841.

Corps of Engineers

Bearwaller Gap Hiking Trail. Length, 6 mi. one way; rating, moderate; elevation change, 300 to 400 ft. This trail is located on Corps of Engineers land surrounding the Cordell Hull Dam and Reservoir, U.S.G.S. quad 321SW, Carthage. To get to the trail from I-40, take exit 258 toward Carthage. You may take Highway 263 to the Overlook trail entrance or take Highway 85 to the Defeated Creek Park trail entrance.

The trail runs from the recreation area to Tater Knob Overlook and is marked with international markings, 3-by-6-inch white painted blazes. It is a unit of both the Tennessee and national recreation trail systems.

Many years ago when the black bear was still common in Tennessee, the bears were often found "wallering" in a patch of woods that offered cool shade and moist earth. The local people have named one of these gathering places "Bearwaller Gap." It is said that the depressions still visible around the gap are all that remain of the days when the bears came here to wallow. There are map brochures and trail registers at the bulletin boards at the trailheads. Ascending the first hill from Defeated Creek Recreation Area, one might observe turkey vultures in the large trees. They are found frequently along this part of the trail. One of the trail's primitive camping areas is located about 0.3 mi. along the trail; no camping permit is required. Potable water is not available at this site.

The trail environment includes many forest types found in Middle Tennessee, including the cedar glade community, unique to the central basin of the state. Hardwood forests in this area are dominated by oaks and hickories; associated species include maple, tulip poplar, ash, dogwood, and redbud. At a point near the Defeated Creek entrance to the trail, a rock outcropping overlooking the trail contains fossils of animals that lived in this area about 300 million years ago when it was under 40 to 60 ft. of ocean. Not far from this outcropping, there is an old stone quarry from which materials were taken for construction of the old Lock 8, completed in 1924. All that remains of the quarry is one steel drilling rod protruding from the rock. It often provides a lookout station for turkey vultures.

Another primitive campsite is located at Two-prong, which is a forked embayment of the lake. There is a spring here, but the water should be purified before drinking. Between Two-prong and the overlook there are many traces of man's early settlement in the area, including old wagon roads, stone fences, and large haystack-shaped piles of stones removed from the fields and pastures to make the land more usable. The Bearwaller Gap Trail is an excellent place to observe wildflowers in the spring, summer, and fall. Some of these are mayapple, red trillium, columbine, cardinal flower, jack-in-the-pulpit, wild geranium, wild phlox, violets, prickly pear, bloodroot, and false garlic. At the overlook end of the trail, the hiker may ascend Tater Knob for an excellent view of Cordell Hull Lake and Dam, the Horseshoe Bend Area, and the Defeated Creek Recreation Area.

Twin Forks Trail. Length, 20 mi.; rating, easy. The trail is located on the East and West forks of Stones River and the backup of J. Percy Priest Lake, where the two rivers join. The trail is on land managed by the U.S. Army Corps of Engineers in Rutherford County. The eastern access is at Walter Hill Dam and Recreation Area on U.S. 231, about 26 mi. south of I-40 at Lebanon or 5 mi. north of Murfreesboro. U.S. 231 is a link in the Trail of Tears State Scenic Route, described in chapter 4. The trailhead is located on the south side of Stones River by an old dam and reservoir in the Walter Hill Park and Picnic Area. There is a second access point at the East Fork Recreation Area, at mile 14 off Central Valley Road, which turns west from U.S. 231 near the trailhead at Walter Hill Park. The western terminus is at Nice's Mill Dam on Sulphur Springs Road. Most of this trail is multiple use, shared by horse and foot traffic. A portion of the foot trail from Walter Hill to the East Fork Area is separated from the horse trail and is better for hikers.

The 8-mi. section of the trail from the East Fork Area to Nice's Mill is used primarily by horse traffic. There are unloading facilities for horse trailers, parking lots, a picnic shelter, and numerous picnic tables scattered in the shade of maple and oak trees at the East Fork Recreation Area. To reach the western trailhead, park on the south side of the river and proceed west along the stream and under the highway bridge. This section follows the line of the river and is marked with white blazes for several miles.

Travelers on the Twin Forks Trail are exposed to a richness of flora and fauna characteristic only of riversides. There are more diverse forms of life here than in any other type of environment. The trail wanders through stands of water-tolerant trees such as cottonwood, yellow poplar, sycamore, and black willow. On the slopes above, a mature hardwood forest composed of hickories, oaks, and maples fights for survival on thin soil with exposed limestone outcroppings. The outcroppings provide good den sites for groundhogs, foxes, bobcats, and skunks—as well as lizards and snakes. The snakes found here include the king, blue racer, garter, and eastern milk snake. There are very few poisonous snakes, but don't rule out the possibility of encountering a copperhead or a timber rattlesnake.

Birds of all kinds can be seen. The bright flashes of the colorful warblers, bluejays, and cardinals are in sharp contrast to the plainly garbed sparrows, thrushes, towhees, and bobwhite quail. As the hiker proceeds down the trail, the king-fishers, great blue herons, and black-crowned night herons croak, irritated at being disturbed from their fishing. Less disturbed are the flycatchers in the upper story of the woodlands—phoebes, pewees, and kingbirds—capturing flying insects. Between the deeper pools, tracks in the soft mud or an occasional crawfish claw indicate where raccoon and mink hunt at night.

If the crawfish escapes the mammalian predators, the backward swimmer must dodge smallmouth and red-eye bass. Farther downstream, where the river gets deeper, there is room for catfish, bream, white bass, rockfish, and carp. The riffles where the raccoon and mink now hunt once witnessed a more dramatic confrontation for survival. The armies of the Confederacy and the Union met a few miles upstream from the terminus of the trail at Nice's Mill. Here, on the West Fork of Stones River near the city of Murfreesboro, a fierce battle (Battle of Stones River) took place, beginning December 31, 1862, with 23,000 casualties. It was the bloodiest single day of the war in Tennessee. The shallow ford at this point was bloody and muddy from the crossing of men, horses, cannons, and equipment as the battle lines were being drawn.

Both armies suffered massive casualties, and on January 2, 1863, the Confederate forces began to retreat, leaving the Union to claim a costly victory. If you are in this area, a visit to the Stones River National Battlefield will provide more information on this battle and a chance to hike on the historical trails there.

Land Between the Lakes

This is a 170,000-acre public outdoor recreation and environmental-education area in western Tennessee and Kentucky containing more than 135 miles of trails in both states, with about one-third of them in the smaller Tennessee portion. Since part of the Tennessee Valley Authority's function is to demonstrate natural resource management and development of recreation facilities, there has been experimentation with various tread materials on the trails. At the campgrounds, bike trails and some hiking trails are paved with asphalt. Bark, gravel, and, more recently, wood chips have been tried as tread-surfacing materials. The 0.5-mi. Songbird Walk at Piney Campground is designed for visitors to observe wildlife, particularly songbirds, and has special plant groups, bird houses, and feeders in a gently sloping field with scattered trees and shrubs. This is a demonstration of wildlife management practices that can be duplicated in a suburban backyard.

North-South Trail, Tennessee Section. Length, 65 mi. with 20 mi. located within the Tennessee portion; rating, easy to moderate. The trail starts at the information center on "The Trace," Tenn. 49, and runs northward past the Buffalo Range to the Kentucky line. It continues through Kentucky to the north visitor's center. There is no camping on the trail, but there are places for backpackers to camp off the trail at various points. The trail is marked by white metal strips. Maps are available at the information center. The trail runs southward from the center parallel to The Trace for about 1 mi., then turns westward for about 2 mi. before turning south again. It winds along the ridge between the Cumberland and Tennessee River watersheds, the Tennessee Valley Divide, for about 6 mi. to the road to Ginger Bay on Kentucky Lake; crossing the bay, it continues south another 2 mi. to the junction with the trail from the Buffalo Range to the Ginger Ridge backcountry camp. From the camp it runs south another mile or so and then swings northeastward through the site of the former town of Model, Tennessee, once famous for moonshine whiskey. The trail crosses the trace and turns northward to the state line.

Two other important LBL trails, the Fort Henry Trails System and the Pawpaw Path, are described in chapters 7 and 10, respectively.

9. Urban Trails

Some of the more challenging, and many of the most interesting, hiking trails in Tennessee are in urban parks. Those described here might be better called suburban trails, since they lie either in sizable natural areas in the suburbs of major cities or on the public lands of smaller towns that support primarily suburban life-styles.

Each of the natural areas of the major cities—Kingsport, Bristol, Knoxville, Chattanooga, Nashville, Jackson, and Memphis—is associated with a nature center featuring a museum and various related facilities for environmental education, ecological research, and ecosystem restoration. Extensive programs of classes, field trips, and projects for volunteers are offered by each nature center to explore and preserve the natural features unique to its area.

In the past decade, or so, many cities in Tennessee began developing truly urban trails in greenways along the rivers or streams important to their historic growth. Notable in this regard are the greenway systems with multi-use trails in Kingsport and Maryville. Chattanooga and Clarksville have built riverfront parks with paved riverwalk trails. Also, Farragut, Knoxville, and Chattanooga have created the initial components of greenway trail systems. Each of these cities has a master plan calling for extension of its greenway and/or riverwalk system. Murfreesboro, Smyrna, Collierville, Savannah (see Trail of Tears, chapter 4), Nashville, and Memphis are in the early stages of greenway or riverwalk projects, while many other communities are proceeding to establish urban trail systems to meet the needs of walkers, joggers, bicyclists, those with physical disabilities, older citizens, and other special populations.

Bristol: Steele Creek Park

There are about 20 miles of hiking trails, rated mainly easy to moderate, in this 2,100-acre municipal park. The park extends along the Beaver Creek Knobs, a forested ridge that starts near Blountville and thrusts northeastward into Bristol's urban heart. This ridge is bisected by the gorge of Steele Creek dammed at the southeast park boundary to back the 53-acre Steele Creek Park Lake up to the northwest park boundary. The park's main recreation area centers around the lake's northern end, where a boat dock and a new Nature Center are located, and it includes two main trails: Lakeside Trail and Tree Walk.

Lakeside Trail. Length, 2 mi.; rating, easy. This hard gravel trail is the most intensively used trail in the park. It is wide enough to accommodate walkers, joggers, and bicyclists and extends from the mouth of the lake to the dam. See chapter 10 for description.

Tree Walk. Length, approximately 0.5 mi.; rating, easy. Interpretive signs featuring trees have been placed at regular intervals along this paved trail, which extends along Steele Creek from The Pines Picnic Area to the footbridge at the mouth of the lake. Also starting in the main recreation area are trails leading into the two more remote sectors of the park, Slagle and Trinkle hollows.

Slagle Hollow Northeast Access Trail. Length, 1 mi.; rating, strenuous. This trail starts across the lake from the boat dock and leads into a complex of trails in the southwest sector of the park centered around Slagle Hollow, which is a registered State Natural Area. Although much of the total 10 miles of trails in this sector is currently used by trail motorcycles, the park's master plan calls for trail planning, reconstruction, and improvement to emphasize hiking usage and reduce motorcycle and other uses inimical to the preservation of the area's sensitive ecology.

Hidden Hollow Trail. Length, approx. 1 mi.; rating, strenuous. This falls within the Trinkle Hollow Boundary Area, which includes the entire section of the Beaver Creek Knobs lying northeast of the lake. It is unspoiled, ecologically significant, and has relatively few trails compared to Slagle Hollow. The Hidden Hollow Trail extends from the Lakeside Trail near the mouth of the lake through a shady secluded hollow up to the highest elevation in the park at the power line cut.

Flatridge Trail. Length, approx. 1.5 mi.; rating, strenuous. It leaves the Hidden Hollow Trail near the bottom and climbs more directly by a number of switchbacks to the same high point, then leaves the power line cut to drop steeply down a ridge to join the Lakeside Trail near the middle of the gorge.

For more information write: Bristol Leisure Services Department, P.O. Box 1189, Municipal Building, Bristol, TN 37621.

Kingsport: Bays Mountain Park

There are 25 mi. of hiking trails in this 3,000-acre nature preserve, with the many individual trails and loops varying in rating from easy to strenuous. There are also 10 miles of unpaved roads designated for mountain bike use. The park, operated by the City of Kingsport, is located just southwest of the city, in Sullivan County west of I-181 and just off Reservoir Road.

Nestled between Holston River Mountain on the northwest and Bays Mountain on the southeast, the park encompasses these ridges and their protected basin, which contains a forty-four-acre lake. Trailhead for the hiking trail system is at the lakeside nature center. There is a $2.00-per-car admission charge for parking and $1.50 charge per person for planetarium and nature programs. Write Bays Mountain Park, 853 Bays Mountain Park Road, Kingsport, TN 37660 for trail map and information.

Knoxville: Ijams Nature Center

Ijams is an eighty-acre city park, bird sanctuary, and community nature center, located on the banks of the Tennessee River in south Knoxville.

On the original twenty-acre tract, easy foot trail loops totaling more than 1 mi. in length wind through mature woods, across meadows and streams, around sinkholes and a pond, and past fern banks and the bluffs overlooking Fort Loudon Lake. An abundant variety of wildflowers, grasses, and native trees and shrubs, along with the aquatic habitats, support a diverse animal population and over forty breeding bird species. Besides the central Serendipity Trail loop, there are the Discovery Trail loop, the Fern Walk, the Pine Succession Trail, and others. With the recent acquisition of an adjacent sixty acres on the lake, a new nature center headquarters and new trails will soon be added. See Chapter 10 for a description of the Serendipity Trail.

To reach Ijams from downtown Knoxville, just follow the green signs from the south end of Gay Street Bridge east on Sevier Avenue and Island Home Avenue. For further information write: Ijams Nature Center, 2915 Island Home Avenue, Knoxville, TN 37920.

Norris: City Watershed

There are more than 20 mi. of interconnecting trails in this large wooded area maintained to protect the water supply. Some of these are jeep roads, but off-road vehicles and "dirt bikes" were barred from the watershed in 1987 at the insistence of the liability insurance carrier. Horseback riders may still use the area. All are good hiking trails. Camping is not allowed, but Norris Dam State Park, nearby, has two good campgrounds. Three very good loop systems are described below.

Cliff Trail, Grist Mill Loop. Estimated distance, 2 mi.; rating, difficult. Most of the Cliff Trail and much of the Grist Mill Trail are on TVA land and are not maintained by the City of Norris. The Cliff Trail starts from the Lenoir Museum at about 900 ft. elevation, follows the face of a cliff overlooking U.S. 441 and the Clinch River up a moderate slope to about 1,000 ft. Plants growing along the trail include Solomon's seal, bloodroot, crested dwarf iris, heartleaf, and others. There are heavy woods above and below. The trail curves left around the end of the bluff and winds uphill past a tiny waterfall on the right, follows the waterway, and branches to the left past a hemlock tree on the right to a shelf at about 1,100 ft. elevation. The trail follows an old roadway around the head of a ravine—a long climb through open woods to the next road—and turns left across a saddle at the end of a real estate development. This part of the trail lies on private property and access cannot be guaranteed. The next intersection, Reservoir Hill Trail at about 1,200 ft., leads left 100 yds. to the Grist Mill Trail back within the City of Norris boundary.

The trail to the left leads to Observation Point. Take the left fork at a dirt pile to loop the 1,380-ft. peak which provides views of a big bend in the Clinch River and Norris Dam upstream to the right. The Clinch River Bridge on I-75 is visible in the distance to the left. The octagonal pavilion at Observation Point was a popular rendezvous for local recreationists until destroyed by vandals; only the stone base remains. A jeep road leads down an easy slope in open woods to the end of the loop, where the Grist Mill Trail goes to the left between twin oaks. The trail follows an old road down a gentle slope, crosses a power line, and turns left beside the line. At another old road about 300 yds. downhill, the trail turns left, still downhill, about 0.3 mi. from the starting point. Hikers might spot a ruffed grouse near the old gristmill, a landmark for visitors to the Norris Dam area.

Clear Creek, Reservoir Hill, Grist Mill Loop. Length, approximately 3 mi.; rating, moderate to difficult. This hike starts from the Grist Mill on the Clear Creek Trail, following the mill stream about 200 yds. to a spring. Clear Creek Road and the creek are below on the left. A bat roost box placed by a TVA biologist is mounted on a tree on the left near the spring. The trail follows a shelf along the side of a steep hill through young timber, passes a rock outcropping, an open spot, then initialed beech trees before curving left across the end of a small ravine. It continues up the creek on a shelf carved out of the hillside for an old millrace. Retaining walls built with hand-cut stones hold the downhill side. The trail passes a weir and pool, crosses a fallen beech tree, and turns left across the road to a footbridge. There is a picnic table on the left past the bridge.

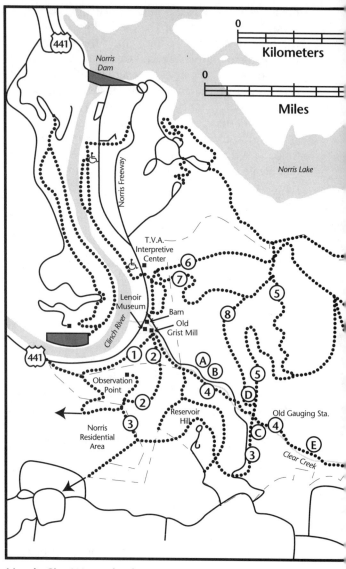

Norris City Watershed

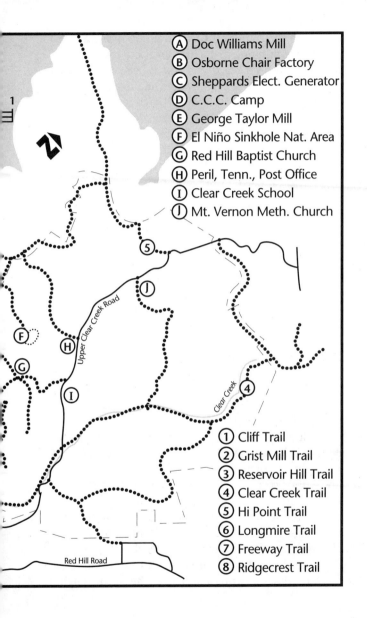

Ⓐ Doc Williams Mill
Ⓑ Osborne Chair Factory
Ⓒ Sheppards Elect. Generator
Ⓓ C.C.C. Camp
Ⓔ George Taylor Mill
Ⓕ El Niño Sinkhole Nat. Area
Ⓖ Red Hill Baptist Church
Ⓗ Peril, Tenn., Post Office
Ⓘ Clear Creek School
Ⓙ Mt. Vernon Meth. Church

Upper Clear Creek Road

Clear Creek

Red Hill Road

① Cliff Trail
② Grist Mill Trail
③ Reservoir Hill Trail
④ Clear Creek Trail
⑤ Hi Point Trail
⑥ Longmire Trail
⑦ Freeway Trail
⑧ Ridgecrest Trail

The trail turns to the right and passes a group of abandoned fish hatchery tanks. Continuing past a dam and pool for the Norris pumping station, it crosses a marshy area and veers left across a small stream flowing through a tile to arrive at the Hi Point jeep road. At the pumping station, Reservoir Hill Trail leads off to the right parallel to Clear Creek Road, heads up a gradual slope 0.3 mi., and crosses the road at a switchback. It climbs the hill on a switchback trail to a brief level stretch, past a sinkhole on the left and a split tulip tree on the right. The trail now leads up a long slope past a picnic shelter on the left, crosses a jeep road, and leads up a steep, straight path to the top of Reservoir Hill, 1,360 ft. elevation. Leaving the picnic area at the underground reservoir, the trail leads to the left downhill about 0.3 mi. under big oak trees, following a long ridge past a footpath on the right. It crosses a power line right-of-way to a junction with a trail leading left downhill to the Norris residential area. Reservoir Hill Trail continues uphill, crossing another power line and curving to the right in second-growth timber. The loop takes the right fork at the next intersection, 100 yds. from the Grist Mill Trail at the twin oak trees. This trail completes the loop back to the old mill.

Clear Creek, White Pine, Ridgecrest Loop. Length, approximately 4.4 mi.; rating, moderate. The loop starts from the picnic table at the pumping station, leaving the Hi Point Road to the east up the left side of Clear Creek on an abandoned roadbed. There is an old weir and gauging station 200 yds. from the start, and water seeps from the hillside on the left another 200 yds. up the trail. The hills on either side flatten and stepping-stones cross the creek as the trail turns up the right side. This portion of the trail is restricted to foot traffic because of its ecological sensitivity. The trail dips into the creek for 25 yds., then makes a slight rise, continuing past a large spring inside a fenced concrete structure to the White Pine Trail 100 yds. beyond. To the right the White Pine Trail follows the access road 0.3 mi. to upper Clear Creek Road.

On the left, the White Pine Trail crosses Clear Creek, much smaller now, and follows a spring branch on the left through a thicket of honeysuckle and multiflora rose into thick woods. It passes an old gauging weir at a spring on the left under a leaning umbrella magnolia and detours around a fallen cedar tree. The trail grows steeper after passing some fallen pine trees. The creek has a solid rock bottom here. After 100 yds. the trail levels off briefly, crosses a thicket in an open area, and then crosses the spring branch, continuing up a gentle slope past a tiny spring with stunted watercress on the left. The flow from a second spring, up the hill, runs down the trail. Springs water the valley floor, encouraging lush growth of weeds and shrubs in the open areas. In the next open spot, Japanese wineberries grow, descendants of an agricultural venture in the 1930s. White blossoms in spring are followed by fuzzy red calyxes that close up around the developing berries. The salmon-colored fruit bursts forth in late June, deepening in color as it ripens. The berry leaves a unique yellow-orange cone when picked. The juicy, slightly tart berries are prized by local residents for making jelly.

Farther up the slope, the waterway dries. At 2 mi. from Clear Creek, the White Pine Trail swings left across a grassy glade, then uphill to open woods. There are more berries, and a bluebird box is mounted on a tulip poplar on the left. The trail drops down across a waterway, then climbs a slope through a timber harvest area. A sign at a fork in the trail, stating NO MOTORIZED VEHICLE TRAFFIC ALLOWED, was often ignored before the area was closed to ORVs. The left fork leads up a steep slope 0.5 mi. to Hi Point Road at 1,460 ft. elevation on the border of Norris Dam State Park. Hi Point Trail leads downhill to the left 0.5 mi. to the cabin area of the park. Our loop follows Hi Point Road to the left past the Longmire Trail to the Freeway Trail, about 0.3 mi., and turns sharply right across the hill at about 1,400 ft. elevation. Temporary roads have been bulldozed to allow access for firewood cutting. The trail forks left downhill on a ridge into a heavy stand of second growth hardwoods and a few scattered mature trees. At 0.2 mi. the Ridgecrest Trail leads to the left.

Ridgecrest Trail leaves the Freeway Trail to the southeast at about 150 degrees, following the top of a ridge. Down a hillside the trail follows an old roadbed to the right past a fallen oak tree, then detours around windfalls, passing under a fallen sassafras before returning to the roadbed. It follows the crest of the ridge down into mixed pine-hardwood forest, becoming steeper down the toe of the ridge. Detouring around old foundations left by a CCC camp and around another windfall, the trail meets another old road that leads left to High Point Road. The starting point at the pumping station is 200 yds. downhill to the right.

Oak Ridge

North Ridge Trail. Length, 7.5 mi.; rating, moderate. This trail follows the north side of Black Oak Ridge along the northern border of Oak Ridge on public greenbelt lands. It was built in the early 1970s by Tennessee Citizens for Wilderness Planning (TCWP), a local conservation organization, with Lily Rose Claiborne as trail committee chairperson. It is maintained by TCWP with the aid of scout troops. In 1973 the North Ridge Trail was the first trail inside a city, the second in Tennessee, and thirty-sixth in the nation to be designated a national recreation trail. It is blazed in white, the access trails in blue. There are eight access points.

Access number 1 is on the right at a yellow barricade, about 1 mi. west of Illinois Avenue (Tenn. 62) on West Outer Drive. The main trail runs to the right off the old Reservoir Road, a former Civil Defense evacuation route, at about 1,100 ft. elevation. It follows the contour along the wooded north side of the ridge about 1 mi., then curves left and drops down to Illinois Avenue at about 1,000 ft. Views of the Cumberlands and Poplar Creek Valley are seen to the north. The trail crosses the four-lane highway, drops down the hill, and follows a county asphalt road to the right, curving right then left around a hairpin turn.

Access trail number 2, the most-used access on the west end, is on the east (right) side of Illinois Avenue about 50 ft. north of the service station at Illinois and West Outer Drive. There is a steep descent about 200 yds. in the wooded greenbelt to the main trail. The main trail leads uphill to the east at about 920 ft., turning sharply left at 100 yds. At another 100 yds. it heads right and follows the 1,000-ft. contour to a power line right-of-way and another view. It crosses the power line, bearing slightly uphill, and enters the woods again at a blazed tree. Following the contour about 0.2 mi., the trail crosses a ravine and climbs back to 1,000 ft. at access trail number 3.

This access begins at the turnaround at the end of North Walker Lane (1,100 ft. elevation) and drops down the hill to the northwest, turning down a spring branch to the main trail. From this intersection the main trail curves northward above the 1,000-ft. contour to skirt an offset in the city boundary, crosses a hill, then drops down to cross a little stream. A gradual ascent follows for 0.5 mi. along a steep hillside before dropping down to access number 4 at Key Springs Road. Key Springs Road intersects Outer Drive on the north side about 0.1 mi. west of New York Avenue, dropping down the side of Black Oak Ridge on a switchback road to the floor of Poplar Creek Valley. The North Ridge Trail crosses the road 0.7 mi. from Outer Drive and 500 yds. south of Tenn. 61, which travels the valley north of Black Oak Ridge.

The trail crosses the road at about 850 ft. elevation, then climbs to 1,150 ft. in deep woods in the next 0.5 mi., passing below a water tower and a television tower uphill on the right. It drops down to cross a ravine and arrives at access number 5, elevation 950 ft. This access is the old Cedar Hill Trail, an abandoned road that starts at the intersection of Orchard Lane and Orkney Road at another yellow barricade. The junction with the North Ridge Trail is about 0.2 mi. down the badly eroded roadway. The main trail leads down Cedar Hill Trail a short distance and turns right, uphill past some striking rock formations.

The trail continues northeast, crossing the old Orchard Trail and ascending to 1,050 ft. past more rock outcroppings. It drops to a small stream and turns up the Georgia Trail to access number 6.

This access begins opposite the end of Georgia Avenue on Outer Drive at a dirt road past a house, dropping over the hill to a ravine and along the spring branch to the junction with the North Ridge Trail. The main trail turns sharply left and climbs a steep grade, 900 to 1,100 ft. in about 0.3 mi., to access number 7, forming part of the Delaware Loop. The Delaware Loop begins on the west side of the city pumping station, slightly west of Delaware Avenue, running northward off Outer Drive. It follows the 1,000-ft. contour about 0.5 mi., then heads westward on the North Ridge Trail to the Georgia Trail and left (east) up a ravine to the starting point.

From access number 7, the main trail runs parallel to the city limits, dropping off to cross a ravine at about 950 ft. and heading back up a hill at 1,080 ft. It crosses another ravine and follows the 1,000-ft. contour about 0.5 mi., crosses yet another ravine, and continues on the contour another 0.3 mi. around the last ravine. The trail ends uphill at access number 8 on the extension of Endicott Lane. Hikers are urged to pay attention to blazes as informal trails have sprung up to connect with other city streets.

Chattanooga: Reflection Riding and the Chattanooga Nature Center

A network of hiking trails, rated easy to moderate, lies within the 300-acre Reflection Riding nature preserve. It starts at the Chattanooga Nature Center and climbs in successively longer loops up the east side of Lookout Creek Valley. Susan's Curves Trail, 1.3 mi., Bradford Williams Trail, 3.5 mi., and the Park Border Trail, 4.2 mi., all wind through predominantly oak forest with scattered pine groves, around deep gorges, across rock fields, and among moss-covered boulders, and they offer occasional vistas of the valley. The Park Border Trail also connects with the Skyuka Trail on Lookout Mountain (see chapter 7). The Great Indian Warpath and the Cisca and St. Augustine Trail crossed Reflection Riding, and in 1863 the Battle of Lookout Mountain began here.

A 3-mile loop for cars starts at the nature center. It features a wide variety of wildflowers in each blooming season, and most trees and shrubs are identified along with many historic points of interest. Walkers find excellent birding here in the early morning hours along wooded areas bordering fields near the creek. See chapter 10 for descriptions of the Woodland Walkway and Wetland Boardwalk trails. A nominal admission charge permits access to the nature center and Reflection Riding.

To reach the Chattanooga Nature Center, exit I-24 at Tiftonia, go east on U.S. 41 2 miles, and turn right on Garden Road which ends at the Center.

Write to The Chattanooga Nature Center, Rte. 4, Garden Road, Chattanooga, TN 37409, for further information.

Sewanee: University of the South

Perimeter Trail. Length, approximately 20 mi.; rating, moderate. The Perimeter Trail is a series of paths following the bluffs around "The Domain" of the University of the South at Sewanee, located on U.S. 64, 4 miles southwest of I-24. Sections along the bluffs expose hikers to many views and lookouts and an abundance of plant and animal life, while those below the bluffs offer access to caves and an impressive array of spring wildflowers. Side trails to Bridal Veil Falls and to Solomon's Temple Cave are particularly rewarding. Some sections of the main trail are also open to horses or mountain bikes.

Points of special interest:
- Bridal Veil Falls—a 30-ft. cascade that falls into a sinkhole indicative of the several caves below
- Morgan's Steep—an excellent sunset view and rock-climbing area
- The Cross—a war memorial at University View
- Old Cowan Highway—the coach road used before U.S. Hwy. 64 was built

- Shakerag Hollow—a wildflower heaven named after an old moonshiner's signal
- Armfield Bluff, Piney Point, Razor's Edge, and Oliver's Rock—popular climbing and rappelling areas

Direct access to the trail with limited parking is available at Morgan's Steep, the Cross, and Green's View. Ample parking at the Lake Cheston recreation and picnic area is less than 0.5 mile by side trail from the junction of the Perimeter Trail and Bridal Veil side trail. The Perimeter Trail offers a multitude of day-hike choices including loops using old fire lanes. Overnight hikes can utilize some areas cleared for primitive camping, or the Forestry Cabin may be reserved through the Forestry Club at the university. For more information write: Sewanee Outing Club, SPO, The University of the South, Sewanee, TN 37375.

Nashville: Percy and Edwin Warner Parks

There are 11 mi. of hiking trails maintained by the Warner Park Nature Center in the 2,665-acre Warner parks. There are also 10 mi. of bridle paths and 30 mi. of paved roads, 6 mi. of which are closed to motorized traffic. This is the state's largest city park entirely within city limits. Its forested core, 80 percent of the total acreage, is a registered State Natural Area. To get to the parks, go south on Tenn. 155 from exit 204 on I-40 to Harding Road, U.S. 70S. Turn right and go to the junction with Tenn. 100. Take the left fork (Tenn. 100) 3 mi. to the Warner Park Nature Center, on the left past Old Hickory Boulevard, for maps and trail information.

The Percy Warner Park trailhead parking lot is in the Deep Well picnic area on Tenn. 100, 1.5 mi. from U.S. 70S. The two trails here are the 2.5-mi. Warner Woods Trail, blazed in white, and the 4.5-mi. Mossy Ridge Trail, blazed in red; both rated moderate. The trails pass through mature woods with huge oaks, tulip poplars, sassafras, sugar maples, hickories, and many others. Wildflowers are abundant spring through fall, and there are many species of ferns, mushrooms, birds, and animals.

There are two trailheads in Edwin Warner Park, one at the nature center, the other at Owl Hollow across the main park drive from picnic area no. 5 off Vaughn Road. Hikers can access the Percy Warner Park trails from the nature center via a 0.8-mi. easy connector trail. Trails are marked with colored arrows on posts at intersections. Three trails are self-guided, with interpretive booklets available at the trailhead. These are the Nature Loop, coded yellow, length 0.75 mi., rated moderate; the Owl Hollow Loop, coded orange, 0.3 mi., rated easy; and the Little Acorn Trail, an easy 150-yd. loop coded green. The Hungry Hawk Trail, coded purple, is an easy 0.3-mi. loop featuring a bird blind, a wildlife tracking station, and a wildlife observation platform. Light green arrows lead to an amphitheater nestled in a clearing. The Harpeth Woods Trail, a 2.5-mi. loop, coded blue and rated moderate, may be started from either trailhead. Hikers can enjoy a variety of forest types and especially large beech, oak, and red cedar trees. Cross an old rock quarry, see fossilized evidence of life forms of 400 million years ago, and enjoy a preserved section of the historic Natchez Trace.

Jackson: Cypress Grove Nature Park

Cypress Grove Nature Park features an elevated boardwalk that winds more than 1.1 mi. through an unspoiled 165-acre cypress forest. Dominant trees in this wetland are white ash, red maple, sweet gum, bald cypress, and water tupelo; jewelweed and cardinal flowers are prominent. There are also open ponds and open meadows in the park that, along with the forest, support a wide variety of wildlife. See chapter 10 for a description of the trails. The park is located on U.S. Hwy. 70 about 1.5 mi. west of the interchange of the U.S. 45 Bypass and U.S. 70 on the west side of Jackson. For information about the park and its special classes, write to Cypress

Grove Nature Park, 866 Airways Boulevard, ATTN: Park Naturalist, Jackson, Tennessee 38301.

Memphis: Lichterman Nature Center

Easy self-guided trail loops, totaling almost 3 mi. in length, wander through this preserve's sixty-five acres of forest, lake, marsh, and field habitats. Nonmember admission fees to the center are $2.50 for adults and $1.75 for students and senior citizens. To reach the park take the I-240 loop in east Memphis to the Germantown/ Poplar Avenue East exit. Go east several blocks on Poplar Avenue, and turn right on Ridgeway Road. Then go several blocks to Quince Road, turn right and go 0.3 mi. to the nature center, on the right. For further information write to The Lichterman Nature Center, 5992 Quince Road, Memphis, TN 38119.

10. Trails for the Handicapped

In 1990 an interim draft of a *Design Guide for Accessible Recreation* was published by the National Forest Service and National Park Service. It estimated that as much as 57 percent of our population has some degree of disability: 37 percent of us with significant long-term physical, mental, or emotional limitations; 10 percent who are elderly or have invisible disabilities such as cardiac or respiratory problems; and 10 percent with temporary disabilities such as broken limbs.

While there are still not enough trails available to the disabled in Tennessee, there are many more with some degree of wheelchair accessibility than there were in 1979, when *Tennessee Trails* was first published. More importantly, recreation planners statewide now recognize the breadth and depth of this need, and existing facilities are being retrofitted, and new projects designed, with the disabled foremost in mind.

The N.F.S./N.P.S. interim design guide uses three accessibility levels to classify outdoor recreation facilities:

- Accessible — Generally, these sites are usable without assistance by all but the most severely disabled.
- Challenge Level 1 — These sites are more difficult for those with limited mobility, and some disabled persons may need assistance.
- Challenge Level 2 — These sites are usable by the more athletic disabled person without assistance, but those with limited mobility will probably need assistance, while use by the severely disabled without assistance is not recommended.

A few of the standards for trails and pathways suggested by the guide, and used in rating the trails described in this chapter, are as follows:

	Accessibility	Challenge Level 1	Challenge Level 2
Grade	5% max.	8.3% max.	12.5% max. not to exceed 200 ft.
Width 1-way 2-way	4 ft. 5 ft.	32-in. min.	32-in. min.
Cross Slope	2% max.	2% max.	3% max.
Surface	Hard	Very firm, compacted	Natural, passable by wheelchair
Distance Between Rest Areas	200–300 ft. max.	100–200 ft. max. where grade greater than 5%	200–300 ft. min. using natural level places where possible

The trails described here are each rated as to overall accessibility based on the above standards for *grade, width, surface,* and *rest areas.* Almost all these trails exceed the 3 percent maximum *cross slope* cited in these standards, at least for short distances in turns. Cross slopes of up to 13 percent are encountered on many of them, and this is noted in the relevant trail descriptions. Each trail surface is also rated as *smooth, fairly smooth,* or *rough.*

All these trails are unobstructed. Most of them have no curbs but are railed at danger spots and on all bridges and elevated boardwalks. The permitted use of each trail, besides wheelchair, is indicated as either *foot* or *multiuse.* The latter includes foot, bicycle, possibly skateboard and rollerblade, but not horse.

Although selected primarily as suitable for handicapped persons, all these trails are interesting and enjoyable for anyone. Some are great jogging trails, and many are particularly attractive for family walks with children.

At the time of our first edition, there were only two trails in Tennessee for persons with handicaps. The Honeysuckle Trail in T.O. Fuller State Park at Memphis was the first of eight "Braille Trails" for the blind designated as national recreation trails across the country between 1973 and 1975. By the mid-1980s, the Honeysuckle Trail had fallen by the wayside from lack of use and maintenance. The Pawpaw Path in the Land Between the Lakes is still in use and is described in this chapter.

Great Smoky Mountains National Park

Sugarlands Visitor Center Loop. This 0.5-mi. accessible, paved foot trail was recently completed. It winds along the West Prong of the Little Pigeon River in the very heart of what is possibly the richest area in North America in terms of the number and diversity of biotic species. A second phase of the project will be the installation of signs, wayside exhibits, audiocassette players, and tactile exhibits. The trailhead is on Newfound Gap Road just south of the visitor center and about 3 mi. southwest of Gatlinburg.

Big South Fork National River and Recreation Area

Leatherwood Ford Walkways. Length, 0.25 mi.; challenge level 2; smooth; foot. This loop beside the Big South Fork River begins at a large trailhead gazebo at the south end of the paved parking area. Accessible rest rooms and public telephone are nearby. From the gazebo the 8-ft. wide paved trail initially drops toward the river on a 16 percent grade for about 50 ft. Here the loop trail turns to the right, downstream, while the trail ahead continues about 200 ft. down a 10 percent grade to the riverside and then across a 300-ft. planked low-water automobile bridge originally built by the WPA. The loop trail goes about 200 ft. downstream, generally level, then again drops on a 16 percent grade for about 30 ft. to an 8-ft.-wide boardwalk. The boardwalk extends another 200 ft. downstream past several riverside observation decks with benches. It then turns away from the river and climbs on a 12 percent grade for about 40 ft. to the paved return leg of the loop which winds back to the trailhead on short up and down grades ranging up to 10 percent. There are cross slopes up to 10 percent in places on the paved trail.

The Leatherwood Ford area is highly scenic and particularly rich in its variety of trees, shrubs, and herbaceous plants. The historic ford itself is named for a locally abundant deciduous shrub with flexible branchlets and tough bark used by native Americans to make bowstrings and baskets.

Leatherwood Ford is on Tenn. 297, 3 mi. east of Bandy Creek Campground. See chapter 8 for location of Big South Fork N.R.&R.A.

John Muir Trail. Length, 0.25 mi.; challenge level 2; fairly smooth; foot. This 4-ft.-wide hard-packed gravel trail starts at the Leatherwood Ford gazebo. Passing under Leatherwood Ford Bridge it leads upstream through northern hardwood (beech-maple) forest with hemlocks, white pines, and yellow birches adding to this northern character. Several rest stops with benches encourage enjoyment of the forest and river. This section of the trail, improved for wheelchair use by the Telephone Pioneers of America, ends at two house-size boulders typical of local gorge streambeds.

East Rim Overlook Trail. Length, 400 ft.; challenge level 2; smooth; foot. An 8-ft.-wide paved trail leads from the paved parking area down two switchbacks on an 8 percent to 10 percent grade through woods of white, red, and chestnut oaks, red maples, and Virginia pines. At the rim of the gorge, a railed wooden platform offers a superb view of the Big South Fork 500 ft. below. Across the river upstream is the mouth of North White Oak Creek gorge. Leatherwood Ford is around the bend downstream. The parking area for this trail is at the end of East Rim Road, which goes west from Tenn. 297 about 1.5 mi. southeast of Leatherwood Ford Bridge.

Land Between the Lakes

The Pawpaw Path. This is a demonstration project, as are many of the facilities in the Land Between the Lakes. Brandon Spring Group Camp, the site of the trail, is not open to the general public, being used for recreational and environmental education, but interested persons can visit the trail by contacting Recreation Services, TVA, Land Between the Lakes, Golden Pond, KY 42231, telephone (502) 924–5602. Brandon Spring is located on Lake Barkley and road 226, about 3 mi. north of the southern boundary of LBL.

The Pawpaw Path gets its name from a small group of pawpaw trees at the south end of the loop. This tree is a member of the custard-apple family occurring in the West Indies. It grows in moist locations in the lower Midwest and the South, though many trees were destroyed when bottom-lands were cleared for agriculture. It has a deep red blossom in spring and bears an elongated yellow fruit with a pleasant aroma, pulpy flesh, and large seeds. The fruit ripens in September and is so highly prized that people seldom allow it to get completely ripe on the tree. It is often called the North American banana because of its shape, but it does not peel like a banana. Most foresters are not familiar with the pawpaw, since it is fairly rare and has no commercial importance.

The Pawpaw Path is actually two loops, the shorter being an asphalt-paved trail about 200 yds. long and fairly flat to accommodate wheelchairs. The longer loop, about 0.5 mi., has a sawdust tread and gentle grades that require moderate effort by heart patients and people who have some difficulty walking. Both loops lie in a shallow basin with a small stream running lengthwise down the middle through open woods. Intersections are designed to "channel" hikers to the right, so that they follow the trail in a clockwise direction. Signs "interpret" the objects of interest along the trail, telling about the trees and their uses and calling attention to groundhog holes and old foundations. A special feature of each loop is tree identification and interpretation. As with the paving, signage is somewhat deteriorated and scheduled for refurbishing by mid-1994.

Trees along the trail include the dogwood, white ash, sweet gum, black gum, oak, hickory, red cedar, wild black cherry, sassafras, tulip, hackberry, beech, and pawpaw. There are ferns, poison ivy, deer browse plants, and wild grapes. The sawdust path leads to the right at about 50 yds. from the beginning of the paved loop. There are benches along the way so that tired walkers can rest and enjoy their surroundings. Footbridges span the brook at the upper end of each loop, and the sawdust path merges with the paved trail just before the bridge at the lower end. The Pawpaw Path is intended to serve as a model for park planners, recreation directors, and environmental educators.

South Cumberland State Recreation Area

Stone Door Trail. Length, 1 mi.; challenge level 1; smooth; foot. See description on page 107.

Long Hunter State Park

Lake Trail. Length, 2 mi.; accessible; smooth; foot. Accessible rest rooms and a public telephone are near the paved trailhead parking area. This 8-ft.-wide paved loop trail winds along the shore of 110-acre Couchville Lake through mixed hardwood and cedar glade forest typical of Tennessee's central basin. The northwest end of the loop crosses the lake on a 300-ft. railed boardwalk. Spring wildflowers, fall colors, wading birds, and waterfowl are the most popular features. Dominant trees such as chinquapin oaks and shagbark hickories are labeled, and interpretive plaques explain other trail features such as limestone sinkholes, a plant succession area, pond ecology, glade forests, and a field-to-forest transition zone.

The steepest grade on the trail is 6 percent in the first 100 ft. from the trailhead. About 200 ft. from the trailhead, a 150-ft. fishing and boat-docking pier is wheelchair accessible, permitting some assisted use of flat-bottomed rental boats by handicapped persons. To reach the trailhead from the park entrance, take the first park road to the left just past the ranger's residence. The road ends at the trailhead parking area. The park is located on U.S. 171 6 mi. south of the Mt. Juliet exit from I-40 (7 mi. east of Nashville).

Meeman-Shelby Forest Day Use Park

Bicycle Trail. Length, 1 mi. (2 mi. R.T.); accessible; fairly smooth; multiuse. The trail is a 16-ft.-wide paved park drive, Piersol Road, now closed to motorized traffic. It starts from the paved parking area at picnic shelter no. 2, where there are accessible rest rooms. The trail extends west along the top of a ridge through tall mature hardwood forest. It ends at a paved circle and picnic shelter on the brow of the Chickasaw Bluffs. Scattered along the trail in grassy openings are seven picnic tables with benches. This is a particularly nice, open but well-shaded trail for wheelchairs and elderly walkers. Cross slopes reach 7 percent to 8 percent for 30 ft., or so, in a couple of gentle curves.

From the paved circle the bicycle trail goes south along the brow of the forested Chickasaw Bluff. Here it is an 8-ft.-wide paved path rated challenge level 1 for wheelchair use for the first 0.4 mi. Toward the end of this section, the grade reaches 7 percent for 200 ft., then 8 percent for a shorter distance, before the trail turns sharply left and drops steeply on switchbacks to the bottom of the bluffs. A warning sign and rail fencing on either side of the trail just before the sharp left turn and steep descent clearly mark the end of the section suitable for wheelchair use.

To reach the trailhead go west from the park entrance, take the first road to the left just past the visitor center, and follow it 1 mi. to picnic shelter no. 2. See chapter 5 for map and location of park.

Steele Creek Park

Tree Walk. Length, 0.25 mi.; challenge level 2; smooth; multiuse. See chapter 9 for location of park and Tree Walk trailhead. This 8-ft.-wide paved trail winds along Steele Creek on rolling grades mostly under 5 percent but up to 10 percent for short distances. It joins the 8-ft.-wide paved Mill Creek section of the Lakeside Trail which extends almost 0.2 mi. up Mill Creek to a paved parking area on Broad Street. This free parking area is the best wheelchair access to the Tree Walk and the Lakeside Trail.

Lakeside Trail. Length, 2 mi.; challenge level 2; smooth to rough; multiuse. From its junction with the Tree Walk, this 8-ft.-wide paved trail drops on a 13 percent grade for about 20 ft. to a 90-ft. railed footbridge (boardwalk) across Mill Creek at the head of the lake. From the end of the bridge, the trail becomes a level 12-ft.-wide hard gravel road with cross slopes up to 5 percent for 20 ft., or so, in a couple of spots. Cobbles protruding an inch or two from the road surface in places can mostly be avoided. There are several benches along this 1.8-mi. section on the grassy strip between the trail and the lake. The steep forested slope on the other side of the trail shades most of the route during the morning hours. Along the way there are great views of the wooded knobs and slopes of the gorge, the lake, and the open landscaped area around the head of the lake.

Nature Center. Length, 0.22 mi.; challenge level 2; smooth to fairly smooth; foot. This recently built facility is expected to open soon. From its paved parking area just off the main park drive, an 8-ft.-wide paved trail leads 500 ft. down a 10 percent grade to a lakeside boathouse. From there a 3-ft.-wide level hard gravel path follows a narrow strip of land across an arm of the lake 400 ft. to the beginning of an 8-ft.-wide railed boardwalk which extends the remaining 300 ft. across the lake to the Slagle Hollow trailhead.

Ijams Nature Center

Serendipity Trail. Length, 0.3 mi.; challenge level 2; fairly smooth; foot. This 4-ft.-wide paved trail loops completely around the broad-topped knoll occupied by the nature center and its country garden setting. On most of the loop, the lower slope is beautifully forested, and many of the native trees adjacent to the trail are identified with braille markers. On a bluff at the apex of the loop, a railed deck with benches overlooks Fort Loudon Lake, and across the trail there is an organic garden. A little farther on a butterfly garden is on the inside of the loop, and limestone sink-holes lie in the forest below. This delightfully varied trail has 10 percent cross slopes in places, one grade at 8 percent for about 70 ft., and a couple of 12 percent grades for about 30 ft. See chapter 9 for location of the center.

Reflection Riding and the Chattanooga Nature Center

Woodland Walkway. Length, 500 ft.; accessible; smooth; foot. See chapter 9 for directions to Reflection Riding. The Chattanooga Nature Center is fully accessible. This 6-ft.-wide paved trail starts at the nature center's paved parking area and leads into the bottom-land hardwood forest of Lookout Creek. It passes a wildlife rehabilitation area where injured creatures such as deer, foxes, hawks, and owls are held in pens for treatment and later release.

   Wetland Boardwalk. Length, 800 ft.; accessible; smooth; foot. This 6-ft.-wide railed boardwalk extends the Woodland Walkway across the forested floodplain of Lookout Creek. It ends on the bank of the creek at a shelter ideally positioned for quiet observation of wetland wildlife.

Drive-through Trail. Length, 0.75 mi.; challenge level 1; fairly smooth; auto and foot. Starting at the nature center parking area, this level part of the 3-mi. hard-packed gravel road loop has mostly pastoral farmland on one side and the bottomland forest of Lookout Creek on the other.

Tennessee Riverpark

Riverwalk. Length, 2.0 mi.; accessible; smooth; multiuse. The Tennessee Riverpark is reached by taking the first exit from Tenn. 153 south of Chickamauga Dam onto Tenn. 58 and taking the first road to the right into the park. This 8-ft.-wide paved trail extends downstream from a parking area below Chickamauga Dam 0.75 mi. to another parking area at the Riverpark headquarters and food concession building. There are accessible rest rooms, telephones, and picnic shelters at each end and two shelters with benches and emergency telephones along the trail. Extensions of the trail at each end past the parking areas and loops through picnic areas add another 1.25 mi. to its length. Most of the route is shaded by large native riverbank trees, and it offers panoramic views of the river. Near the lower end parking area, a paved railed 6-ft.-wide ramp descends about 300 ft. on a 7 percent grade to a railed fishing pier that extends 50 ft. over the river beneath the DuPont Parkway Bridge. Long-range plans call for a connector trail via this bridge between the Riverpark and the North Chickamauga Creek Greenway (see page 173).

Bluff Walk. Length, 0.5 mi.; challenge level 1; smooth; multiuse. This second phase of the Tennessee Riverpark was completed in 1994 and lies almost 6 mi. downstream from the first, described above. It begins at Ross's Landing Plaza at the corner of Chestnut Street and Riverfront Parkway in downtown Chattanooga. In 1815 John Ross established a landing, warehouse, and ferry here. A 6–8-ft.-wide paved and railed trail extends upriver on both sides of the Parkway from the Tennessee Aquarium at the Plaza to an outdoor amphitheater beneath Walnut Street Bridge. It then climbs via a series of accessible paved, railed switchbacks past the Bluff Furnace historical site to the Hunter Museum on the blufftop. Here it connects with the south end of Walnut Street Bridge, a 100-year-old steel-truss structure. Formerly a two-lane automobile span, it is now a 1,600-ft. linear pedestrian park offering many inviting rest spots with superb views of the city's dramatic river and mountain setting.

A phased master plan calls for extending the riverpark upstream from Hunter Museum to the completed handicapped-accessible Rowing Center and then beyond to connect with the first phase. Later phases will develop the riverpark downstream from Ross's Landing to Moccasin Bend, where the 22-mi. Riverwalk will end in a broad loop opposite the north end of Lookout Mountain.

North Chickamauga Creek Greenway

Greenway Trail. Length, 0.35 mi. O.W., 0.7 mi. R.T.; challenge level 2; smooth; foot. The North Chickamauga Creek Greenway, and the trail, extend about 1.5 mi. along the east side of the creek from near Chickamauga Dam to Spangler Farm. To reach the greenway parking area, exit Tenn. 53 just north of Chickamauga Dam onto Lake Resort Drive and go east about 0.2 mi. to the greenway entrance on the left. Accessible rest rooms and emergency telephone are located at the parking area. This 8-ft.-wide paved trail starts at the north end of the parking area and proceeds upstream paralleling the creek. First crossing a slightly arched 70-ft. railed bridge, it climbs steadily through second growth hardwood forest at grades up to 8 percent for 200 ft., or so, and up to 10 percent for shorter distances. Cross slopes reach 6 percent at several points. At 0.35 mi. from the trailhead, the Lower Loop Trail branches off to the right and returns 0.35 mi. to the trailhead. The Greenway Trail continues straight ahead another 0.35 mi., where it ends as a paved trail by making a 0.2-mi. loop. From near the end of the loop, an 8-ft.-wide gravel trail continues 0.6 mi. over the top of a high bluff (with a good view of Lookout, Elder, and Signal mountains) to Spangler Farm a city/county owned facility. Unassisted wheelchair use of the Lower Loop Trail and the last 0.35 mi. of the paved part of the Greenway Trail is not recommended because of grades up to 17 percent on the former and up to 21 percent in a tight turn on the latter.

Edwin Warner Park

Riverbend Road. Length, 0.2 mile; accessible; fairly smooth; multiuse. This 16-ft.-wide paved half-loop, closed to motorized traffic, begins at the picnic area 6 parking lot just off the main park drive from the Vaughn Road entrance. It follows the inside of a bend in the Little Harpeth River with the wooded riverbank on one side and closely mowed open woods and meadow on the other. This is a good spot for early morning wildlife watching. Snapping turtles, banded water snakes, raccoons, muskrats, and green and great blue herons are often seen along the river. Kingfishers regularly work the bend, and red-tailed hawks often soar over the meadow. Squirrels, bluebirds, and a variety of other songbirds can usually be seen or heard.

Interior Road System. Length, 5 mi.; challenge level 2; smooth; multiuse. This former scenic drive system of 16-ft.-wide paved roads is permanently closed to motorized traffic. It was resurfaced in mid-1993 to a 10-ft. width leaving 6 ft., or so, of the old pavement to eventually deteriorate to a soft track. The system consists of: a 2.5-mi. main loop that winds at midslope completely around the forested hilly spine of the park; a 0.6-mi. interior loop around a high point with a scenic view of the Harpeth Valley; a 0.14-mi. connector road across the main loop; and four roads from 0.2 to 0.4 mi. long connecting the main loop with the park perimeter.

One exterior connector road on the south side of the park starts from a gate at a parking lot near picnic area 8, which has soon-to-be-accessible rest rooms. Another exterior connector road on the north side of the park begins at a gate near the paved parking area just inside the Tenn. 100 (Woolwine) entrance to the park. All gates barring auto access to the interior road system have 4-ft.-wide unobstructed openings.

The exterior connector roads and the interior road system all have grades mostly 5 percent or less but also have long stretches (up to 300 ft.) from 6 percent to 8 percent and many shorter segments (up to 50 ft.) from 9 percent to 13 percent. Cross slopes throughout the system are often over 3 percent, and in the numerous sharp turns commonly range from 10 percent to 14 percent.

The main loop begins and ends at two gated former entrances to the park 0.05 mi. apart on Old Hickory Boulevard. There is limited parking space at the more northerly of these entrances, and here a relatively flat and especially scenic 0.46-mi. section of the main loop begins. It goes north along a contour of a spur off the park's central spine, then rounds the end of the spur and goes south along almost the same contour. The steep slope above is in mature hardwood forest and the lesser slope below, mostly open meadow. Around the end of the spur, mossy stonework of the WPA era extends along both sides of the road. Here the road enters a deep wood on both sides where large gnarled beech trees cling to almost precipitous rocky slopes. This is the only spot on this section where grade and cross slope reach 10 percent for about 30 ft. Here, where the wood begins on the lower slope, a large accessible observation deck at the edge of a meadow overlooks the nature center and the valley of Vaughn Creek. See chapter 9 for directions to Edwin Warner Park.

McGregor Park

Cumberland Riverwalk. Length, 1,700 ft.; accessible; smooth; foot. This 12-ft.-wide paved trail extends along the landscaped bank of the Cumberland River from a playground to a boat ramp with adjacent parking areas at both ends. Along the trail are picnic areas and three river overlooks. Soon a 700-seat amphitheater will be built into the riverbank as well as a rivermaster's house featuring an accessible Cumberland River interpretive center. Long-range plans envision extending the riverwalk to a 2.5-mi. length. McGregor Park is located in Clarksville on Riverside Drive (U.S. 41A Bypass) which extends from U.S. 41A on the north to the junction of Tenn. 12 and Tenn. 13 on the south.

Cypress Grove Nature Park

Boardwalk. Length, 1 mi.; accessible; smooth; foot. About 80 percent of the trail system is a 6-ft.-wide railed elevated boardwalk. The Jewelweed Trail is an unelevated boardwalk, 4 ft. wide and unrailed. The only significant grades in the system are 100 ft. at 8 percent from the parking area to the nature center and 40 ft. at 10 percent where the Jewelweed Trail first leaves the main boardwalk. Sensitive fern and royal fern are prominent along the Jewelweed Trail, and a Wildlife Rehabilitation Center is under construction nearby. From the railed observation deck at Killdeer Pond, one sees black willows, cattails, bulrushes, and, in late summer, blooming meadow beauty and water primrose. Cypress Knee Loop circles an area thick with these protuberances, and it provides benches and a shelter. An observation deck and a tower on Wood Duck Lake offer good places to watch songbirds, waterfowl, wading birds, owls, and raptors. Overall this is a delightful trail at any season for the sights, sounds, and smells of typical West Tennessee cypress-tupelo swamps. See chapter 9 for location of the park.

11. Trails on Private Land

A number of the trails described in this guidebook cross private land but were built by state personnel and volunteer organizations. The trails described in this chapter were built by private industry on its own lands. Bowater Incorporated Southern Division owns more than 350,000 acres of timberlands in Tennessee. In 1967 Bowater adopted an open-land policy and published maps of three of its tree farms to be used by outdoor recreationists. The largest recreation complex is on the Piney River Tree Farm near Spring City. It includes the Piney River Picnic Area, Stinging Fork Falls Pocket Wilderness, Newby Branch Forest Camp, and the Piney River and Twin Rocks trails.

Next the company decided to set aside small areas of unique character and outstanding scenic value, accessible only by foot trails. The first of these "pocket wildernesses," Virgin Falls, was dedicated in 1970. In 1969 the first trail was developed at Stinging Fork Falls, later included in a pocket wilderness. There are now four of these areas in Tennessee, and all are state-registered natural areas.

An attractive booklet, complete with maps, on Bowater recreation opportunities may be obtained by writing to the Public Relations Department at Bowater Incorporated Woodlands Division, Calhoun, TN 37309-0188.

Piney River Tree Farm

The general area contains three Bowater trails, two of which start from the Piney River Picnic Area. To reach these trailheads, turn west off U.S. 27 onto Tenn. 68 in Spring City, then left on Shut-In Gap Road at the western edge of town; a sign points to Walden Ridge. It is about 1 mi. to the picnic area. Pennine USGS quad, 118NW.

Twin Rocks Nature Trail. Length, 2.5 mi.; rating, moderate. This short trail winds up a narrow ridge formed by a horseshoe bend in Piney River. Starting at the picnic area (about 850 ft. elevation), it parallels the Piney River Trail a short distance, then breaks away to climb through a dry rocky area covered with oaks and hickories. It winds around the north face of a steep slope through dense laurel to an intersection with the return trail, which drops off the ridge to the west. The trail to Twin Rocks continues along a narrow backbone carved out of the rest of the ridge by the Piney. Panoramic views of the Great Valley of the Tennessee and Piney River Gorge are spectacular along the ridge, especially from the top of Twin Rocks, 1,360 ft. elevation. Ruffed grouse and other birds common to the region are often heard along the trail. The return trail intersects with the Piney River Trail for the return to the picnic area.

Piney River Trail. Length, 10 mi.; rating, easy. This trail was dedicated as a national recreation trail April 22, 1978; 230 people registered for the dedication hike and received the official trail patch. Starting at the picnic area at 850 ft. elevation, it winds up the hillside to about 1,100 ft. following the contour. Twin Rocks Nature Trail branches off to the left as the Piney River Trail rounds the end of the ridge. At 0.8 mi. a side trail leads downhill to the river. One-half mile farther it crosses a branch, holding closely to the contour. After the second branch the trail leads downhill to the 102-ft. suspension bridge across the river, 3 mi. from the picnic area.

Across the bridge, the trail turns upriver on the bed of an old narrow-gauge Dinky railroad that was used to mine and log the area beginning in 1909. The hiker can still see an occasional rail, a broken axle, an old mine site, and remnants of the old grade. Spots along the creeks—Hemlock Falls, White Pine Cascades, Raining Bluffs Falls, Wonder Log Falls—add a great deal of beauty to the trail experience. A 20-ft. creosoted bridge runs over Pine Branch, and a 50-ft. steel bridge crosses Rock House Branch. One-half mile up Rock House Branch, named from the overhanging rocks that provide shelter from the elements, is a tiny pool called the "bathtub." The stream has carved a deep basin in solid rock, not much larger than a bathtub, 7 ft. deep.

Up Duskin Creek from Rock House Branch, there is a 50-ft. steel bridge across a slide area. At Big Cove a mixed hardwood forest has grown in the moist soils, rich from clear cutting in the Dinky Line days. Picking its way around a bluff, the trail passes an old mine tipple and its waste pile on the right. Beyond, another 50-ft. steel bridge crosses to the south side of Duskin Creek. (All materials for the bridges were flown in by helicopter to avoid destruction of the sites.) A short distance upstream the trail crosses a road and turns north to the Newby Branch Forest Camp. It is 6 mi. back by road to the Piney River Picnic Area. The one-way hike from Piney River Picnic Area to Newby Branch Forest Camp takes five to six hours.

Stinging Fork Trail. Length, 3 mi.; rating, moderate. The last of the trio in the Piney River Tree Farm, this trail was built in 1969, the first trail on Bowater property. The parking area is on the right, 4 mi. from the picnic area on Shut-In Gap Road. The soft needles from a managed pine plantation cushion the hikers' feet as the trail meanders toward the edge of Stinging Fork Gorge. It follows the edge through thickets of huckleberry bushes and laurel. The huckleberries are ripe and abundant in early summer, and the laurel is in bloom. A spur trail leads down a narrow point to a rocky promontory called Indian Head Point, where there is a view of the rugged Stinging Fork Gorge. The main trail drops down to a series of steps and switchbacks to Stinging Fork Creek below the falls. A short trip up the creek finds Stinging Fork Falls, a 35-ft. waterfall and cascade located in a very picturesque setting. At present the trail just runs in and back, but future plans include development of a loop trail in the area.

Laurel-Snow

Laurel-Snow Trail. Morgan Springs USGS quad, 110SE. Length, 8 mi.; rating, moderate. This trail is located near Dayton, Tennessee, site of the famous "monkey trial" of the 1920s, when a high school science teacher John T. Scopes tested the Tennessee law prohibiting the teaching of the theory of evolution in the public schools. The trial attracted Clarence Darrow for the defense and William Jennings Bryan on the side of the fundamentalists. Bryan College was established in Dayton as a memorial to the "silver-tongued" politician. The corner drugstore where Scopes and friends worked out the idea of the test case is still there. The store has been remodeled, but the old-fashioned soda fountain tables were retained.

To get to the Laurel-Snow trailhead, turn west off U.S. 27 just north of the Rhea County Hospital and follow the signs about 2 mi. to the pocket wilderness parking area. This was the first national recreation trail in Tennessee and the first in the nation to be designated on private land by the U.S. Department of the Interior. From the parking area at about 850 ft. elevation, the trail follows an old nineteenth-century railroad bed up Richland Creek Gorge and past an old mine tunnel on the right. It crosses a 50-ft. bridge over Laurel Creek at 1,100 ft. and forks, the east leg going to Laurel Falls, some 80 ft. high, and to Bryan Overlook with its view of the Tennessee Valley at 1,700 ft. elevation. The west leg goes up the other side of the gorge to Buzzard Point, which provides a view of the Tennessee Valley and Dayton. Doubling back on this leg across a spur of the Cumberland Plateau, the trail winds down to Snow Falls, a small waterfall in an extremely rugged gorge on Morgan's Creek.

A few remnants of the early twentieth-century mining operations remain, such as railroad ties, bridge foundations, a closed air shaft, and rock retainer walls. For the most part, though, the area has returned to its natural wild state, with little evidence of man's use during the past fifty years. Just south of the parking area are some old coke ovens almost covered with vegetation.

While the trail is not classified as difficult, covering it in its entirety is a good day's workout. The round trip on the Laurel Falls option alone is 5 mi. and requires three hours, while that on the

Snow Falls option is 6 mi. and requires four hours. It is a popular outing spot for Bryan College students, who affectionately refer to the area as "the pocket."

Virgin Falls

Virgin Falls Trail. Lonewood USGS quad, 332SE. Length, 8 mi.; rating, difficult. This trail is located 8 mi. south of De Rossett off U.S. 70 between Crossville and Sparta. Follow a county road 5.9 mi. and turn right on the access road at the Chestnut Mountain Wilderness sign. Located on the Caney Fork River in White County, Virgin Falls was the first Bowater's pocket wilderness trail to be opened with a formal dedication hike in May 1970. This is a single trail with a loop at the end. It is recommended that six to eight hours be allowed for the full round trip. The access trail leaves the parking area at about 1,750 ft. elevation, passing mostly through typical Cumberland Plateau second-growth timber. It follows down a branch to Big Branch Falls at 1,700 ft. and drops on down to cross Big Laurel Creek at 1,540 ft. The trail follows the right side of the creek downstream.

At 1,500 ft., a side trail leads to the right to the Caney Fork Overlook Loop, rising along the hillside to 1,700 ft., where there are views of the Caney Fork River Valley to the south. The overlook trail drops back to the main trail at 1,300 ft. The main trail veers to the right along the 1,300-ft. contour to cross a branch, then turns left along the hillside, and drops to 1,100 ft. The spur trail to Big Laurel Falls is to the left. At Big Laurel Falls the creek disappears underground beneath a 30-ft. waterfall. An overlook near Big Laurel Falls provides a view of Caney Fork Valley with no signs of man visible. The main trail now runs westward along the side of a steep bluff overlooking the Caney Fork River about 0.5 mi., then turns north up Little Laurel Creek at the beginning of the Virgin Falls Loop. The trail drops gradually along the side of a ravine for about 0.3 mi. to Sheep Cave where a stream emerges. It crosses Little Laurel Creek at about 1,000 ft. elevation, doubles back south, then curves west across a point to Virgin Falls.

At Virgin Falls, an underground stream surfaces on the side of a sinkhole, runs over a flat rock surface for 50 to 75 ft., then drops 110 ft. over a cliff, disappearing into another cave at the bottom. This is a year-round stream. Sheep Cave is geologically similar except the stream is smaller. The caves have been mapped, and information on them is available from the Tennessee Division of Geology. Leaving the falls, the trail continues southward around the head of a ravine, winding down to Little Laurel Creek at about 880 ft. elevation. A designated backpack camping area is located off the trail to the right. The main trail continues eastward, climbing back to about 1,050 ft. to complete the loop. From here, backtrack on the main trail to the parking area.

North Chickamauga

Opened to the public in June 1993, this new 1,100-acre pocket wilderness contains two trails and features mature forest, interesting rock formations and spectacular vistas, wildflowers and wildlife, old coal mines, and an abandoned moonshine still. The parking area is located off U.S. 27 on Montlake Road just beyond the city boundary of Soddy-Daisy and just before Montlake makes a hairpin curve to begin the ascent of Walden Ridge. The entrance area features picnic facilities and handicapped accessibility to North Chickamauga Creek. Chattanooga USGS quad, 105SE.

The Hogskin Branch Loop Trail leads northwest from the parking area and is 1.5 miles round trip. The Stevenson Trail extends along the north slope of North Chickamauga Creek from the northwest end of the Hogskin Branch Loop. Including the northern leg of the Hogskin Branch Loop, the Stevenson Trail is about 4 miles long or 7.8 miles round trip. Both trails are rated easy to moderate, and a primitive camping area is located near the end of the Stevenson Trail.

12. Trail Organizations

Tennessee Trails Association. Organized in 1968, this statewide association is dedicated to the development of a state trails system. There are three types of membership: individual, supporting, and student. The association works with the Department of Environment and Conservation on right-of-way acquisition, trail development, and maintenance, and it sponsors the Adopt-a-Trail program. There are monthly membership activities, and TTA publishes a monthly newsletter. Five or more members in one location may form a local chapter. There are chapters in Nashville, Memphis, Murfreesboro, Cookeville, and Clarksville. For information, write to Tennessee Trails Association, P.O. Box 41446, Nashville, TN 37204.

Smoky Mountains Hiking Club. Organized in 1924, this is the oldest and largest independent trail club in Tennessee. SMHC has published an annual handbook since 1927 and has been affiliated with the Appalachian Trail Conference since 1929. The club sponsors thirty-five to forty hikes a year, plus two slide shows and other social events, and publishes a monthly newsletter. It maintains more than 100 miles of the Appalachian Trail. For more information, write to them at P.O. Box 1454, Knoxville, TN 37901.

Tennessee Citizens for Wilderness Planning. The group was organized in 1966. It is a conservation activist organization that includes trails in its overall program. It sponsored the building of the North Ridge Trail in Oak Ridge (described in chapter 9) and oversees the maintenance of this trail, in cooperation with the City Parks and Recreation Department and local scout troops. It has an agreement with TVA and Hiwassee Land Company to maintain the Whites Creek Small Wild Area Trail on Watts Bar Lake. It maintains the Cedar Barrens Natural Area, including an interpretive trail, in Oak Ridge. For information contact Liane B. Russell, Newsletter Editor, 130 Tabor Road, Oak Ridge, TN 37830, (615) 482–2153.

Tennessee Eastman Hiking and Recreation Club. The group is made up of employees of Tennessee Eastman Company. The club maintains 115 miles of the Appalachian Trail and helped establish the Trail of the Lonesome Pine. For information, write to the club in care of Tennessee Eastman Company, P.O. Box 511, Kingsport, TN 37662.

Historical Hiking Trails, Inc., and **Shiloh Military Trails, Inc.,** P.O. Box 17507, Memphis, TN 38187-0507. They publish *Hiking Trails of America* jointly with Boy Scout Troop 343 of Memphis "for Boy Scouts, Girl Scouts, and other youth groups." The organizations sponsor patch awards for nineteen trails, seventeen of them in Tennessee, and publish materials about Shiloh National Military Park, Memphis Historical Trail, and other places of historical interest. Ken Humphreys is responsible for the success of many of the projects sponsored by these groups. Award sponsors for other trails in Tennessee are listed in *Hiking Trails of America.*

Tennessee Recreation Trails Advisory Board. The board was created in May 1993 by the Tennessee Department of Environment and Conservation in compliance with the Symms National Recreational Trails Fund Act of 1991. It supersedes the ad hoc State Trails Council of Tennessee and is comprised of twenty members chosen by the department from among nominees submitted by all user groups wishing to participate. The twenty members include two from each of the following user groups: hiking, horse, water-based, bicycle, all-terrain vehicle, off-road motorcycle, four-wheel drive, physically challenged, and multiple use trails. Also, there is one representative each for runners and for walkers. The chairman is Mr. Ed Cole, Ass't Commissioner, Tennessee Department of Environment and Conservation, 21st Floor, L&C Tower, 401 Church Street, Nashville, TN 37243.

Tennessee Chapter of the Sierra Club, P.O. Box 5152, Kingsport, TN 37663. Groups are located in the Tri-Cities, Knoxville, Chattanooga, Nashville, and Memphis. Each group has monthly meetings and a year-round program of outings and activities related to environmental protection.

The Nature Conservancy Tennessee Field Office, 2002 Richard Jones Road, Suite 304-C, Nashville, TN 37215; **The Tennessee River Gorge Trust, Inc.** 300 James Building, 735 Broad Street, Chattanooga, TN 37402; and **The Southern Appalachians Highlands Conservancy** P.O. Box 4092 CRS Station, Johnson City, TN 37602. Each of these organizations is engaged in preserving and protecting ecologically significant natural areas in, respectively, Tennessee, the Grand Canyon of the Tennessee River in Hamilton and Marion counties, and the Highlands of Roan in Carter County and adjacent North Carolina counties. Each works in partnership with government and private landowners to assure protection of such areas on their lands, and each also acquires and manages such areas when no other means to assure protection is available. Finally, each has a program of outings and ecosystems-protection projects for its members and supporting volunteers.

References

The titles listed below may be of interest to the region's hikers.

Brandt, Robert S. *Tennessee Hiking Guide.*

Brewer, Carson. *Hiking in the Great Smokies.*

Coleman, Brenda D., and Jo Anna Smith. *Hiking the Big South Fork.*

Homan, Tim. *Hiking Trails of the Joyce Kilmer-Slickrock and Citico Creek Wilderness Areas.*

Manning, Russ. *The Historic Cumberland Plateau—an Explorer's Guide.*

Manning, Russ, and Sandra Jamieson. *Best of the Big South Fork.*

———. *The Best of the Great Smoky Mountains National Park.*

———. *South Cumberland and Fall Creek Falls.*

Murless, Dick, and Constance Stallings. *Hikers Guide to the Smokies.*

Skelton, William N. *Wilderness Trails of Tennessee's Cherokee National Forest.*

About the Author

Evan Means, the son of a country editor, was himself a journalist for fifty years. An outdoor conservation writer with numerous published articles, he is the founder of the Southeastern Outdoor Press Association (SEOPA) and a past president of Outdoor Writers Association of America (OWAA). Outdoor editor at the *Oak Ridger* (Tennessee) for four decades, Means also managed to pursue a career in electrical engineering and write two plays. He originated the Cumberland Trail in 1965 while president of the Clinch and Powell River Valley Association. The trail was chosen as the pilot project for the Tennessee Trails Association, which Means cofounded in 1968.

He was the first recipient of the Tennessee Trails Award, presented by the Tennessee Trails Association in 1979. He received the Z. Carter Patten Award, the highest honor given by the Tennessee Conservation League, and was made a life member of SEOPA in 1981. He was awarded honored life membership in the Tennessee Outdoor Writers Association in 1983. He received the Ham Brown Award, the highest honor bestowed on a member of OWAA, in 1982. He was the first recipient of the Tennessee Trails Association Lifetime Recognition Award in 1992.

He served on the board of directors of the National Trails Council from 1980 to 1986 and was president of the Tennessee Trails Association in 1975 and 1984. He received the Tennessee Outdoor Writers Association award for the best newspaper feature written in 1983 and for the best newspaper news article written in 1984.

About the Editor

Bob Brown is a trustee of the Tennessee field office of The Nature Conservancy. He was the first president of the Tennessee Trails Association and currently serves on the Tennessee Recreation Trails Advisory Board, the Metropolitan Nashville Greenway Commission, and the board of directors of the Friends of Warner Parks. He is a longtime member of most of the organizations listed in chapter 12.

Also of Interest from the Globe Pequot Press